The Literature Review

The Literature Review

A Step-by-Step Guide for Students

Diana Ridley

2nd Edition

Los Angeles | London | New Delhi
Singapore | Washington DC

Los Angeles | London | New Delhi
Singapore | Washington DC

SAGE Publications Ltd
1 Oliver's Yard
55 City Road
London EC1Y 1SP

SAGE Publications Inc.
2455 Teller Road
Thousand Oaks, California 91320

SAGE Publications India Pvt Ltd
B 1/I 1 Mohan Cooperative Industrial Area
Mathura Road
New Delhi 110 044

SAGE Publications Asia-Pacific Pte Ltd
3 Church Street
#10-04 Samsung Hub
Singapore 049483

Editor: Katie Metzler
Assistant editor: Anna Horvai
Production editor: Ian Antcliff
Copyeditor: Rosemary Morlin
Proofreader: Louise Harnby
Marketing manager: Ben Griffin-Sherwood
Cover design: Wendy Scott
Typeset by: C&M Digitals (P) Ltd
Printed and bound by
Ashford Colour Press Ltd

© Diana Ridley 2012

First published 2008. This edition 2012

Library of Congress Control Number: 2011944017

British Library Cataloguing in Publication data

A catalogue record for this book is available from the British Library

ISBN 978-1-4462-0142-8
ISBN 978-1-4462-0143-5 (P)

Contents

List of tables and figures

Acknowledgements

I would especially like to thank the authors of the theses and dissertations whose work appears in the book. In particular, I would like to acknowledge Ruth Bacigalupo, Emma Coveney, Dawn Culverson, Hannah Fairbrother, Ling Feng, Ei leen Lee, Analeen Moore, Morgan Meyer, Dino Ovcina, Key-young Son, Ian Watson and Thomas Webb.

My thanks also go to the organisations and people who have given permission to reproduce material: EndNote (Thompson Reuters), Google Inc., ScienceDirect, Chris Hart, Jerry Wellington, David Huffaker, Sandra Calvert, Ken Hyland, Nicholas Groom, Jennie Popay, Paul Thompson and Étienne Wenger.

I am also grateful for the editorial support provided by Sage, in particular from Patrick Brindle, Anna Horvai, David Hodge, Ian Antcliff and Katie Metzler.

About the author

Diana Ridley is currently a Senior Lecturer at the TESOL Centre, Sheffield Hallam University, UK where she is the course leader for the MA TESOL programme. She supervises both masters and doctoral students in the fields of English language teaching and academic literacies as well as teaching on both undergraduate and postgraduate degree courses. Prior to her role at SHU, Diana was an English teacher in Spain and a teacher trainer in Tanzania. She has also taught English as an additional language in both the primary and secondary sectors in the UK and English for Academic Purposes in a number of UK universities. At the University of Sheffield, she developed and delivered a thesis writing course for doctoral students as part of a wider research training programme. Her own PhD research was in the area of academic literacies, focusing on the role of the literature review in postgraduate research writing and the journeys that research students travel when working on this aspect of their studies. Her teaching and research interests are in discourse and genre analysis, sociolinguistics, English as an additional language, academic literacies and qualitative research methodologies.

1

Introduction

'The first thing you must do is conduct a comprehensive literature review.' This is one of the early tasks that many research students are asked to undertake by their supervisors. It can sometimes be frustrating, when you are keen to make a start on researching a particular problem that you have identified, to be advised to go and search for relevant work done by others, to identify pertinent theories, or just generally to read around the subject. However, it *is* important to explore the field in which you are going to do your research and gain a thorough awareness and understanding of current work and perspectives in the area so that you can position your own research clearly on the academic map of knowledge creation. An essential aspect of academic research is that it has connections with the work of others.

'But where do I start?' and 'What exactly is a literature review, anyway?' are common questions. The literature review is an activity which has many facets and it is not unusual to feel somewhat baffled when trying to work out exactly what is expected. To be tackled successfully, it requires thoughtful organisation and planning from the beginning. Before embarking on the challenge it is therefore helpful to give careful consideration to the following questions in the context of your own discipline:

- What is a literature review and what purposes does it serve in relation to your research?
- Why is it such a vital component of research?
- What are the various ways it can be realised in a dissertation or thesis?
- What does the process of completing a literature review involve?

I begin to address these questions here and elaborate further on the ideas throughout later chapters. The book as a whole contains:

- extensive practical tips on how to prepare, organise and write your review successfully;
- extracts from a variety of different sample dissertations and theses to illustrate the points being suggested;
- tasks for you to do which involve observations and analysis of the dissertation and thesis text extracts and reflection on a range of aspects of your own research and literature review.

It can therefore be used as a self-study guide and either read from start to finish at the beginning of the research process to give you a comprehensive view of what is entailed or relevant chapters can be visited as you progress through your research. I would, however, recommend reading Chapters 1 to 5 as you begin the reading for your research because they focus on strategies for conducting efficient searches of the literature, and techniques for reading efficiently and organising the information you collect. Chapters 6 to 10 will become more pertinent when you prepare to write your review and will continue to be relevant as you draft and revise your work. Chapter 11 is a new chapter in this edition and discusses the purposes and processes involved in conducting a systematic literature review. This type of review differs from a thesis or dissertation literature review in that it is a stand-alone investigation usually conducted by a team of experienced researchers. The majority of the book, however, assumes that you are a student conducting research for an undergraduate, masters or doctoral programme or a supervisor of a student undertaking such research.

After working through the guide, I hope that you will have extended your awareness of the issues involved and be able to navigate your way through the maze of identifying and efficiently reading the pertinent literature, and then writing an effective literature review which blends in with your own research.

In this initial chapter, I define the term 'literature review'; discuss the significance of the literature review in research; and suggest alternative ways that the literature review can be positioned in the final draft of a dissertation or thesis, giving the contents pages of dissertation and thesis case studies as examples.

What is a literature review?

When attempting a definition of this complex phenomenon, it is helpful to break it down into two parts: first, the finished *product* of the literature review which appears in the final draft of the dissertation or thesis, and second, the *process* that is involved in conducting a review of the literature.

The 'literature review' is the part of the thesis where there is extensive reference to related research and theory in your field; it is where connections are made between the source texts that you draw on and where you position yourself and your research among these sources. It is your opportunity to engage in a written dialogue with researchers in your area while at the same time showing that you have engaged with, understood and responded to the relevant body of knowledge underpinning your research. The literature review is where you identify the theories and previous research which have influenced your choice of research topic and the methodology you are choosing to adopt. You can use the literature to support your identification of a problem to research and to illustrate that there is a gap in previous research which needs to be filled. The literature review, therefore, serves as the driving force and jumping-off point for your own research investigation.

The term 'literature review' also refers to the process involved in creating the review that appears in your dissertation or thesis. It is an ongoing activity which begins when you pick up the first book or article related to your research and continues until the day you finish the final draft. Initially, your literature review helps you to formulate your research questions; at the same time, you begin to identify the relevant theories and related research studies to your own and the methodology that you might adopt for your research. Later, the literature assists you in the analysis and interpretation of your data. This book explores all aspects of the process including literature search strategies, systems for storing your key sources and notes, reading strategies, and techniques for writing the review.

Some additional definitions of the literature review from other authors are given below to show the varying emphases that different study guides put on its role and purpose.

> Literature reviews should be succinct and ... give a picture of the state of knowledge and of major questions in your topic area.
>
> (Bell, 2010: 112)

> [A literature review can be defined as] the selection of available documents (both published and unpublished) on the topic, which contain information, ideas, data and evidence written from a particular standpoint to fulfil certain aims or express certain views on the nature of the topic and how it is to be investigated, and the effective evaluation of these documents in relation to the research being proposed.
>
> (Hart, 1998: 13)

Typically, the literature review forms an important chapter in the thesis, where its purpose is to provide the background to and justification for the research undertaken.

(Bruce, 1994: 218)

[The purpose of the literature review] is to locate the research project, to form its context or background, and to provide insights into previous work.

(Blaxter et al., 2010: 124)

[A literature review should] demonstrate … a fully professional grasp of the background theory to your subject.

(Phillips and Pugh, 2010: 64)

[In a literature review a writer] extracts and synthesises the main points, issues, findings and research methods which emerge from a critical review of the readings.

(Nunan, 1992: 217)

[The literature review should be] a coherent argument that leads to the description of a proposed study.

(Rudestam and Newton, 2007: 63)

From these definitions and quotes, we can see that the literature review serves many different purposes and entails a wide variety of activities. It is therefore not surprising that it may seem a formidable task – particularly at the beginning. However, a thoroughly researched and well-written review can be both an exciting and a rewarding experience.

The literature review at different degree levels

Chris Hart (1998: 14–25) summarises the differences in the characteristics of a literature review at different levels of study and outlines the criteria for a successful review. Table 1.1 is taken from his book *Doing a Literature Review: Releasing the Social Science Imagination.*

Jerry Wellington et al. (2005) discuss the professional doctorate and the role of the literature review, in particular in relation to the EdD thesis. They suggest that a literature review for an EdD degree is likely to be more professionally oriented than for a PhD thesis. It is also likely to be shorter as the

TABLE 1.1   Degrees and the nature of the literature review

Degree and research product	Function and format of the literature review in research at these levels
BA, BSc, BEd project	Essentially descriptive, topic focused; mostly indicative of main, current sources on topic.
	Analysis is of topic in terms of justification.
MA, MSc, MPh dissertation or thesis	Analytical and summative, covering methodological issues, research techniques and topics. Possibly two literature-based chapters, one on methodological issues, which demonstrates knowledge of the advantages and disadvantages, and another on theoretical issues relevant to the topic/problem.
PhD, DPhil, DLitt thesis	Analytical synthesis, covering all known literature on the problem, including that in other languages.
	High level of conceptual thinking within and across theories. Summative and formative evaluation of previous work on the problem. Depth and breadth of discussion on relevant philosophical traditions and ways in which they relate to the problem.

Source: Hart, 1998: 15

usual length of an EdD thesis is about 50,000 words, in comparison to approximately 70–80,000 words in a PhD thesis.

It is also relevant to mention here that there are other types of literature review which are not undertaken as a stepping stone for a piece of primary research. I'll refer to these two main alternatives as: 1) a stand-alone review and 2) a systematic literature review (see Chapter 11). A stand-alone review is a self-contained literature review on a particular topic which could be conducted for an undergraduate or postgraduate module assignment (e.g. a review on learner autonomy for an education assignment). An entire dissertation or thesis could also be a stand-alone review if it involves an in-depth critical exploration of the literature in a specific area as opposed to being a project including primary data collection and analysis. On the other hand, as mentioned earlier in this chapter, a systematic review is not usually part of a student's assessed degree work. It is a professional and rigorous undertaking which synthesises findings from a sizeable number of individual studies on a topic often with a view to informing a policy or health treatment. Search strategies, article selection, and synthesis and analysis of data are all documented and transparent. I discuss this process in more detail in Chapter 11.

The main focus in this book is on a literature review which leads into a research project for a university degree programme and the final written version appears usually as a chapter or chapters in a dissertation or thesis. Bearing in mind the differences highlighted in Table 1.1, there are some general

LITERATURE REVIEW

principles which can be applied to the process of doing a literature review at all levels and for all degree types, and it is the intention of this book to provide such guidance and suggestions on practice.

Why is it important to undertake a literature review as part of your research?

When you first decide on the problem you think you want to investigate for your research, you may not be thinking extensively about the wider context. But your research is a small piece in a complicated jigsaw puzzle; it does not exist in isolation. It is dependent on what others have done before and you will contribute to an ongoing story or debate. Your reader therefore needs to know about the whole jigsaw puzzle and not simply the shade and shape of your particular piece. In a literature review, you are contextualising your work; you are describing the bigger picture that provides the background and creates the space or gap for your research.

Where do we find the literature review in a dissertation or thesis?

The literature review often appears as a distinctive chapter or a group of chapters in the final draft of the dissertation or thesis. The titles for these chapters vary and can often be topic related instead of being called 'the literature review'. However, it is also possible that the literature review may be integrated throughout the whole thesis and a single chapter is not identifiable. In the latter case, it does not mean that a literature review has not been completed as it is an integral part of all research. The researcher has simply chosen to use the related literature in a more integrated way throughout the thesis. This approach is particularly likely to be the case in research which is based on an analysis of texts and documents as is the case in the fields of history, English literature or biblical studies. Although the extracts from dissertations and theses shown in this book are from identifiable 'literature review' chapters, the guidance offered is also relevant for the integrated literature review as the processes which can be adopted are similar.

How the literature review may be integrated in different theses where there are identifiable literature review chapters and/or sections is illustrated below. There are two main approaches: *dedicated* and *recursive*. In the first approach, the literature review is included in a chapter or series of chapters, frequently with topic-related titles, near the beginning of the thesis. It often begins in the introduction and continues in one or more subsequent chapters. In some fields

Example 1.1 Contextualising your research

A doctoral student in a School of East Asian Studies at a UK university, Key-young Son, was conducting research into President Kim Dae-jung's Sunshine Policy in South Korea. He was investigating strategies of engagement with North Korea and theories of state identity changes which have enabled relations between North and South Korea to improve. He wrote an extensive literature review (the contents page appears below). In a thesis consisting of eight chapters (363 pages), the literature review extended over three chapters and was 144 pages in length (40 per cent of the thesis).

In the first literature review chapter, he explored the political theories of 'containment' and 'engagement' in relation to the Cold War. In the second chapter, a theoretical framework for his thesis was established based on the concept of 'comprehensive engagement'. And in his final literature review chapter, he described the historical context for his study by giving an overview of the changing relationship between North and South Korea. This theoretical and historical overview created a context in which to situate the detailed investigation of President Kim Dae-jung's Sunshine Policy in South Korea between 1998 and 2003.

Key-young shows in detail where his research is positioned within the field of research on International Relations. He does not simply tell his reader about the particular events in the Korean Peninsula's history which relate to the Sunshine Policy. He explains the theories he is using to interpret the events and gives a historical overview of the significant events which have created the context in which the Sunshine Policy was implemented.

eg →

Contents

Chapter 1: Introduction

1.1 Introduction

1.2 Research Questions and Objectives

1.3 Hypotheses

1.4 Approach, Methodology and Contribution

1.5 The Structure of the Thesis

Chapter 2: Containment and Engagement

2.1 Introduction

(Continued)

Example 1.2 Contextualising your research

The following example is from an MPhil to PhD transfer paper. This is a report which is an integral part of the PhD process for the majority of doctoral students at UK universities. The transfer or upgrade paper (it is known by a variety of different names in different universities) is usually submitted approximately one year after starting on a full-time research degree programme. It typically takes the form of an extended research proposal and outlines the background, aims and research questions, significant and relevant literature, and the proposed methodology of the PhD research. It serves as a milestone when both tutors and the student can reflect on and assess progress and decide whether the student is ready to proceed with the research on a PhD programme.

In this example, Hannah is conducting research in the area of children, food and health. The study has been prompted by a concern with childhood obesity. After a brief introduction where she introduces the topic of obesity and children's eating practices (see contents page below), Hannah includes the literature review in the second section. It is 39 pages in length out of a total of 71 for the whole paper, i.e. it comprises 55 per cent of the report. The literature review is divided into six sub-sections including an introduction and conclusion. The four main content sections discuss and critically analyse literature from a range of disciplines all of which inform Hannah's research on children's perceptions and understandings of health and food.

In the first section, Hannah introduces her theoretical approach to research with children by exploring the literature which argues that the child's voice and perspective is essential. Then, she synthesises research on children as consumers, and identifies a need for further work investigating how children interpret the different messages around them in a range of media and social contexts. After this, she reviews empirical studies which have reported on children's perspectives on food and highlights their limitations; by doing this, Hannah begins to pave the way for her own focus. Finally, the significance of socio-economic position is explored.

Through a critical analysis of the literature under these four headings, Hannah has created a context for her own study and positioned herself as a particular type of researcher in relation to research with children. She has drawn attention to key issues, such as children as consumers and socio-economic position, which will underpin her investigation. She has also emphasised the limitations in previous empirical studies in the field to justify the need for her own.

Contents

1. Background

    1.1 The childhood obesity epidemic

(Continued)

Source: Fairbrother, 2010: iii–iv

such as medicine, the complete literature review may appear as part of the introduction under suitable headings and subheadings. Many doctoral theses, in particular, are made up of a number of different research studies which although independent, are connected by the overarching umbrella of the research topic. In these cases, the second approach is more appropriate, with the literature review likely to reappear at various points in the thesis. It begins in the introduction and then continues at the start of each chapter which presents a different study or group of studies. The different areas covered in the literature review for each study are generally referred to in the thesis introduction where the overall background to the research is provided. Examples of both organisational approaches, taken from the contents pages of PhD theses and an MA dissertation, illustrate the various ways in which the literature review can be integrated into the whole thesis (see Examples 1.1–1.7).

Approach 1: Dedicated chapter or chapters to the literature review

In Examples 1.1 above and 1.3 below the literature review appears in a chapter or series of chapters with topic-related titles near the beginning of the dissertation or thesis. Example 1.2 above and Examples 1.4 and 1.5 below illustrate how there is a dedicated chapter immediately after the introduction which actually has the title 'Literature Review'.

Example 1.3 A dedicated group of chapters to the literature review

Ei leen Lee conducted research in the field of sociolinguistics looking at language shift and language revitalisation among speakers of a specific Creole which is used within a small community in Malaysia. (A creole is a language in its own right which has its origin in extended contact between two or more different language communities. The creole incorporates features of each of the original languages.) Ei leen's literature review begins in Chapter 1, the introduction, with the background historical context of the language, the community where the Creole is spoken, and the national policies which have affected its use. She examines the findings of previous research studies in the field and explains how her research is different from and extends previous research on this particular language. In Chapter 2, she discusses the relevant theories and concepts related to language shift and maintenance which underpin the research and examines three different approaches to the study of language shift in linguistic minority communities. In the third chapter, she explores theories for 'reversing language shift' and considers the role of language planning in the process of revitalisation of endangered languages. These three chapters provide the background which then lead into the description of the methodology, data collection, findings and conclusions.

Contents

Chapter 1: Introduction

Source: Lee, 2003: iv–vii

Example 1.4 A dedicated single chapter to the literature review

In this example from a PhD thesis in the field of education, Ling Feng explores curricula for education for sustainable development in both China and the UK through three higher education case studies. As well as having a dedicated chapter with the title 'Literature Review', her integration of the literature begins in the Introduction where she clarifies how she is using key terminology for her research: education for sustainable development and the curriculum; she highlights the urgency of sustainable development issues in both the UK and China; and she justifies her research in relation to higher-education institutions, sustainable development and cross national research. For all of these purposes, she cites sources to support her arguments.

In the second chapter, the literature review, she explores the concept of Sustainable Development in much greater depth and gives an international historical overview; the theme of curricula is debated by examining four important curriculum perspectives in relation to Education for Sustainable Development; she discusses the current contexts in Chinese and British Higher Education Institutions with regard to Education for Sustainable Development; and the significance of knowledge sharing between countries. She draws on three of the curriculum perspectives discussed to provide the theoretical underpinnings for the case study research which follows in subsequent chapters.

Contents

Chapter 1: Introduction

    1.1 Background of the research

    1.2 The research questions and design

    1.3 The justification of the research

    1.4 Outline of the thesis

Chapter 2: Literature review

    2.1 Introduction

    2.2 The notion of sustainable development (SD)

Source: Feng, 2010: i–iii

Example 1.5 A dedicated single chapter to the literature review

This example is from a masters dissertation in the field of second language learning. Analeen Moore was researching the influence of formal pronunciation instruction on the English pronunciation of a group of adult German students. Her literature review appears as a single chapter after the introduction and before she begins to describe her experiments in the subsequent chapter. She starts off the review by giving a historical overview of the changes in emphases that pronunciation instruction has received in the field of English as a foreign language (EFL) teaching, and then moves on to define the term 'comfortable intelligibility', which is important when considering target pronunciation. She subsequently examines the effects of instruction, first on second language learning generally and then, more specifically, on the improvement of pronunciation in the target language. In the final part of the review, she defines the features of pronunciation that are analysed in the study when looking at the developments in the pronunciation of the learners in the sample.

eg →

Contents

Introduction

Chapter 1: Literature Review

    1.1 Historical background

    1.2 Target pronunciation and intelligibility

    1.3 Research into the effects of instruction

        1.3.1 Second language research

        1.3.2 Pronunciation research

    1.4 Specific features of pronunciation

        1.4.1 Strong and weak forms of words

        1.4.2 Contractions and elision

        1.4.3 Assimilation

        1.4.4 Liaison

        1.4.5 Stress

        1.4.6 Intonation

    1.5 Summary

Chapter 2: The experiment

Source: Moore, 2001: iii–iv

Approach 2: A recursive literature review

When a thesis consists of a number of different research studies, the literature review is likely to begin in the introduction and then continue at the start of each of the different studies. The reviews before the individual research studies generally elaborate in more detail on the topics raised in the introduction.

 Example 1.6 A recursive literature review

This example is from a PhD thesis in the field of psychology for which a series of different studies were conducted to investigate how people self-regulate their behaviour in order to achieve their goals. There were nine research studies in total, which were grouped in four chapters (Chapters 2 to 5). In the introduction, the author begins to discuss previous research and theories related to the regulation of behaviour: goals, motivation and implementation intentions. In subsequent chapters, these areas are revisited in more detail; for example, in Chapter 2 he elaborates on the theories of behavioural intentions and in Chapter 3 more detail is given on goal-achievement models. As before, in the example contents page shown below, a number of the more detailed subheadings have been omitted.

Contents
Chapter 1: Introduction
    1.1 The influence of goals on behaviour
        1.1.1 Behavioural intentions
        1.1.2 Unconscious goal pursuit
    1.2 The intention-behaviour 'gap' and the problem of volition
    1.3 Implementation intentions
        1.3.1 Accessibility of the specified cue
        1.3.2 Strength of the cue-behaviour association
    1.4 Plan of the thesis
Chapter 2: Meta-analysis of intention-behaviour relations
    2.1 Behavioural intentions as the cause of behaviour
    2.2 What other variables influence whether intentions cause behaviour?
    2.3 Study 1
        2.3.1 Method
        2.3.2 Results

(Continued)

Example 1.7 A recursive literature review

In this example from the field of civil and structural engineering, the researcher completed three different studies in the area of groundwater contamination, each of which has each been published separately in a peer-reviewed journal. These appear in Chapters 2, 3 and 4 of the PhD thesis. The literature review was visited briefly in the Introduction (Chapter 1) and then elaborated on in further detail in the introductions of the three chapters (Chapters 2, 3 and 4) which describe the different research investigations. In this thesis, the different parts of the literature review are fairly concise and there are no headings and subheadings within the introductions to identify different topics within the literature review. However the adapted contents page below gives an idea of how the review is spread over the three different pieces of research. (Please note, detailed subheadings under 'Method and modelling procedures', and 'Results and discussion' have been omitted from the original in the example below.)

Contents

Chapter 1: Introduction

    1.1 Background

    1.2 Objectives

    1.3 Scope of work

    1.4 Structure of thesis

Chapter 2: Modelling kinetic processes controlling hydrogen and acetate concentrations in an aquifer-derived microcosm

    2.1 Introduction

    2.2 Method and modelling procedures

    2.3 Results and discussion

Chapter 3: Insights gained through multispecies field scale reactive transport modelling driven by biodegradation complexity

    3.1 Introduction

    3.2 Modelling methods

    3.3 Results and discussion

    3.4 Conclusions

(Continued)

(Continued)

Chapter 4: Advantages of using adaptive remeshing in parallel for modelling biodegradation in groundwater

4.1 Introduction

4.2 Model formulation

4.3 Test cases

4.5 Multi-dimensional field scale simulations

4.6 Advantages of parallel processing

4.7 Advantages of sparse matrix storage approach

4.8 Advantages of adaptive remeshing

4.9 Conclusions

Chapter 5: Conclusions

Source: Watson, 2004: 4–6

Structuring your literature review

The above examples of contents pages show how different writers position their literature reviews within the doctoral thesis or masters dissertation and how they break down the related literature into themes or topic areas. As your reading and research progresses, you will find that you gradually begin to categorise your own work in this way, with the final organisational structure and fine-tuning of your literature review being decided by the focus of your research. This process is examined in more detail in Chapter 6.

 Task 1.1 Choosing a literature review approach

Ask your supervisor to recommend two or three recently completed dissertations or theses in your discipline. After looking at these examples, answer the following question.

Which of the alternatives for positioning the literature review within a dissertation or thesis, described in this chapter and listed below, seems to be most common in your field?

- The literature review is a distinct chapter or chapters near the beginning of the thesis or dissertation.
- The literature review is introduced in general terms in the introduction and revisited in more detail at the beginning of different research studies in the dissertation or thesis.

- Reference to the related literature is interspersed throughout the whole thesis or dissertation and there is no specific literature review chapter.

Now think about your own research topic.

As a way of helping you choose which alternative may suit your own work, think about the advantages and disadvantages for each alternative in relation to your own topic.

As your work progresses consider which alternative you are most likely to adopt for your own literature review and dissertation or thesis. What are your reasons for making this choice?

 Summary

To summarise, this initial chapter has considered:

- the overall definition of a 'literature review';
- a consideration of different types of literature review;
- the literature review's importance in relation to postgraduate research;
- where the literature review may be positioned in the final draft of a doctoral thesis or masters dissertation.

Overview

This introductory chapter has set the scene for the more detailed aspects of the literature review which are examined in the chapters that follow. In Chapter 2, we look further at the multiple purposes of a literature review with extracts from theses and dissertations to demonstrate how the different purposes can be achieved. In Chapters 3, 4 and 5 we consider a range of up-to-date strategies for efficient information searching, evaluating source material, reading and note taking, keeping records, organising source material, and avoiding plagiarism and copyright infringement. Chapter 6 reflects on the writing process and how one can go about organising and structuring the information in a literature review. Referencing conventions are explored in Chapter 7, with coverage of the way references are integrated into the text and how they appear in the bibliography. There is a discussion about the meaning of plagiarism and some examples of the practices that constitute plagiarism. We also consider disciplinary differences in citation patterns and styles. In Chapters 8 and 9, we reflect on what it means to be critical in a literature review and think about techniques for foregrounding writer voice when integrating sources into one's writing. Chapter 10 discusses the importance of constant revisions and updates of a literature review. We consider the links that are likely to arise between a literature review undertaken at the beginning of the research process and the analysis of the data and discussion of implications arising from your own work. Finally in Chapter 11, the process of conducting and critically appraising a systematic literature review is explored. As part of this discussion, we clarify the differences between a dissertation or thesis literature review and a systematic literature review.

This guide can be used as a reference tool throughout your research, with you visiting particular chapters at the time they are most relevant to you and your work. The chapter aims are clearly stated at the beginning of each chapter to enable you to identify the parts that you need at different stages of your research. Alternatively, you can read the book in its entirety to gain an overview of the whole process. Whichever approach you adopt, the suggestions and examples given should provide you with a basis on which to conduct your own literature review and decide how it can be most effectively integrated into your dissertation or thesis.

2

The multiple purposes
of a literature review

Chapter summary

In Chapter 1, a number of different definitions of the literature review were given. In essence, its function is to show how related work in the field shapes and influences your research. The aim is to use the literature selectively and creatively to provide a stimulus for your own work.

This chapter provides:

- a more detailed discussion of the specific purposes of the literature review;
- a selection of extracts from various dissertations and theses to illustrate how these purposes are realised in a cross-section of research contexts;
- a framework to help prompt your thinking about the important elements of your own literature review.

The multiple purposes

When considering the content to include in your literature review, it is important to reflect on the purposes which you wish to address when including references to the work of others. The multiple purposes of the literature review which appears in your thesis or dissertation can be categorised as follows:

- it provides a historical background for your research;
- it gives an overview of the current context in which your research is situated by referring to contemporary debates, issues and questions in the field;
- it includes a discussion of relevant theories and concepts which underpin your research;
- it introduces relevant terminology and provides definitions to clarify how terms are being used in the context of your own work;
- it describes related research in the field and shows how your work extends or challenges this, or addresses a gap in work in the field;
- it provides supporting evidence for a practical problem or issue which your research is addressing, thereby underlining its significance.

The precise nature of your research will determine which of these purposes receive greater emphasis in your own literature review, but it is important to give each one careful consideration when deciding what your review should encompass.

Some of the functions listed above may be realised in the introduction to a thesis or dissertation instead of in an actual literature review chapter. In Chapter 6, the relationship between the introduction and the literature review is considered in more depth and the purposes which are more likely to be partially or completely fulfilled within the introduction are specified. In a review which is integrated throughout the whole thesis, references to the related literature fulfil the purposes listed above as and when appropriate in the body of the text.

Additionally, in relation to the methodology adopted for your research, you will draw on the literature to justify your choice of a particular approach to the research and the research methods. The references cited can also provide support for the specification and size of the sample you select to be your data, and the sites chosen for your data collection. This particular purpose of the literature is likely to appear in a methodology chapter. Therefore, when we talk about multiple purposes of the literature review, it is important to adopt a flexible approach to the location in the dissertation or thesis where each one is addressed.

As stated in Chapter 1, it is important to show that you have a thorough understanding of the field and that your review of the literature is not a 'laundry list' (Rudestam and Newton, 2007: 62) of previous studies. Essentially, you are building up an argument which leads into your research; and as you develop your argument you draw on source texts selectively to provide support for your assertions. By demonstrating ownership of the argument, you show not only that you are knowledgeable about the field but also that you are entering into a dialogue with other researchers in your field, that is, you are joining a community of researchers in your area. An essential feature of a successful argument in a literature review is that you make connections between one reference and another, and also explicit links between these sources and your own work. The process of developing your argument in greater detail is also discussed in Chapter 6.

The extracts included below, from a range of academic fields and disciplines, illustrate some of the different purposes that the literature can serve and at the same time show how the writer in each case is building up his or her arguments. You will notice that in many situations, a combination of different purposes can be fulfilled in the same part of the text, although, in my presentation of each example, I have focused on the predominant purpose. The choice of examples is intended to provide snapshots of the different purposes being realised rather than a full picture of each of the literature reviews cited.

Historical background

Your research will almost certainly be situated in a context which has a history. For example, it may be important to describe the sequence of events or policy changes which have led up to the current situation in which your research takes place. Or you might include an account of the development of the research field itself, which documents how knowledge has progressed and perspectives have changed in relation to your topic. As part of the historical background, it may be significant to highlight differing interpretations of events, policies and research findings.

Example 2.1 Historical background

Taken from the field of town and regional planning, this example focuses on the background to contemporary theoretical debates in planning policy. The researcher provides a historical context for the research, situating it against the backdrop of post-war planning and the general stance taken among postmodern theorists.

eg → Disenchantment and disappointment with the results of British post war planning have inspired a 'post-modern' reaction that has sought to reconsider contemporary planning practice, and dominates current theoretical debate. Although those belonging to this post-modern school of thought varied in their approach, most regarded today's planning 'disasters' as the result of an overly authoritarian system which dictated a singular, narrow world view onto society (Harvey 2000). The post-modern theorists were instead concerned for planning to

(Continued)

25

(Continued)

realise its full democratic potential by recognising and engaging with difference, recognising that there was not one singular 'public', but many publics with different life-experiences (Healey 1992a, 1992b, 1998; Forester 1989; Campbell and Marshall 2002). There was a concern then with the particularities of individual places, a fascination with local knowledge and cultures (Harvey 2000) and a general foreboding of any universal principles.

Source: Adapted from Coveney, 2003: 5

In a similar way to Example 2.1 above, Example 1.1 in Chapter 1 sets the scene historically for research situated in the post-Cold War period in East Asia. There the researcher creates a historical context for the work in Chapters 2 and 4, entitled 'Containment and Engagement' and 'Historical Overview of the Korean Divide: structure and norms' respectively.

Example 2.2 Historical background

Example 2.2 includes two extracts from a section entitled 'Historical review of education for sustainable development' which is a part of the literature review from the thesis already cited in Example 1.4 in the previous chapter. In this section, Ling reviews the origins of the term, 'education for sustainable development' and also discusses how interpretations and implementations have changed in recent decades.

eg → The evolution of sustainability education has incorporated the significant influence of some of the eighteenth and nineteenth-century thinkers, writers and educators, notably Goethe, Rousseau, Humboldt, Haeckel, Froebel, Dewey and Montessori (Palmer, 1998). Nationally and internationally, Scottish Professor John Smyth is recognised as one of the founders of environmental education (EE), which was both one of the first terms used in relation to sustainability education and one that remains in common usage. He combined his deep interest in nature with his belief in the benefits of education, particularly its ability to bring about change in human thinking and actions, which took him onto the international scene. He participated in writing the first internationally accepted definition of EE which was presented at the International Working Meeting on Environmental Education in the School Curriculum convened by the International Union for Conservation of Nature (IUCN) and UNESCO in 1970 ... (IUCN 1970).

Source: Feng, 2010: 26–7

The term sustainability education officially emerged from the World Summit on Sustainable Development (WSSD) in 2002 as a more inclusive, humanistic version of EE. Having revealed that the goals laid out in the Earth Summit ten years before were still far from becoming reality, the WSSD in Johannesburg identified a clear need to rethink education, and sustainability education paved the way for this 'rethinking' (UNESCO Bangkok, no date). UNESCO (no date) defines sustainability education as 'learning how to make decisions that balance and integrate the long-term future of the economy, the natural environment and the well-being of all communities, near and far, now and in the future' (no page). According to UNESCO (2004), 'the ultimate goal of sustainability education is to empower people with the perspectives, knowledge and skills for helping them live in sustainable societies' (no page).

Source: Feng, 2010: 29

Example 2.3 Historical background

This example comes from the field of health-related research and describes the way that children have traditionally been viewed in society and for research purposes. Later, Hannah goes on to challenge the framework.

eg → Children have traditionally been viewed as objects or 'sociological projects' in the study of child health (Christensen 2004; Mayall 1998). Adult or 'adultist' perspectives have dominated research agendas with three main consequences (Christensen 2004) ... This view of children and its consequences for the research agenda in child health reflected a broader picture within what has been termed the 'dominant framework' for understanding children (James and Prout 1997, p. 10).

The 'dominant framework' has its roots both in sociology and developmental psychology. Working from a sociological perspective, Parsons (1956) highlighted children's need to be socialised to gain an awareness of cultural values and conventions, an empty vessel waiting to be filled with knowledge from adults. Piaget (1955), using a cognitive-developmental theory of growing up, viewed children as lacking in the necessary rationality to make sense of the world. Lee (2001, p. 42) notes:

> The dominant framework endorses the treatment of children as a special case of humanity. It portrays children as peculiarly malleable and ties this malleability to an incompleteness that stems from their proximity to 'nature' and their lack of self-possession.

Source: Fairbrother, 2010: 5–6

Contemporary context

The coverage of the contemporary context in which your work is situated is likely to centre on current topics of debate in the field and the direction of recent and ongoing research. This part of your literature review will link quite closely to the discussion of the significance – and therefore the justification – of your own work.

Example 2.4 Contemporary context

In this extract, the researcher provides the reader with an introduction to the topic of groundwater contamination and current research in the area, within the civil and structural engineering field. This contextualisation also serves to highlight the significance of his topic by giving the reader a sense of why it is important to study different ways of reducing groundwater contamination.

eg → Reactive transport modelling of groundwater systems has become an important field of research during recent years (e.g. Zheng and Bennett 1995; Steefel and MacQuarrie 1996; ... Mayer et al. 2002; Prommer et al. 2003). One reason for this is that it is a potentially powerful tool in understanding processes which contribute to the cleansing of contaminated groundwaters. At the field scale, the risk arising from groundwater contamination may be reduced by natural processes (natural attenuation) (Carey et al. 2000; Lerner et al. 2000), or by various engineered remediation methods (Page 1997; ... Wagner et al. 2002). Biodegradation is a major process contributing to removal of contaminant mass in plumes of groundwater pollution, and at most field sites is a very significant natural attenuation (NA) process (Smets and Pritchard 2003). Contaminant removal by biodegradation is also preferable to contaminant retardation by, for example, sorption processes, since the mass may be transformed to non-toxic products, as against being stored up for possible later release into the flowing groundwater.

Source: Watson, 2004: 12

Example 2.5 Contemporary context

The following extract gives an overview of the current issues and debates in connection with information management in the National Health Service in the UK. It provides an introduction to the research context of information management in the National Health

Service and, at the same time, defines some of the relevant terminology used in the current study.

eg → Information management in the NHS (National Health Service) has been described as 'health informatics'. This concept is applied to support clinical research, decision-making and practice (NHS Executive 1999). Information management in health care is 'central to ... all aspects of information handling in patient care and management of health care services' (O'Rourke 1999: 1). Health informatics emphasizes the use of information technology to manage and provide health services (MacDougall and Brittain 1998). This is quite different to the wider definitions of information management that I have mentioned previously (for example, Best 1996; Parsons 1996; Davenport 1997). These holistic definitions of information management put technology on the periphery, emphasize human involvement and take into account the whole information environment.

MacDougall and Brittain (1998) outlined recent developments and trends in health information. They divided health information into four types: scientific, clinical and health services information; patient-generated clinical data; corporate activity management information; and information for patients, carers and the public. The literature regarding information management can be discussed under the headings, strategies, problems, achievements, needs and resources.

Source: Bacigalupo, 2000: 28

Example 2.6 Contemporary contexts

This extract from the field of child health illustrates the current debate around different paradigms for research with children. It follows on from Example 2.3 above in the previous section which presented the 'dominant framework' as the paradigm that had historically been assumed to be the norm for childhood research. Hannah summarises and interprets the 'new paradigm' which challenges the 'dominant framework', before introducing a further critique which highlights limitations and weaknesses of 'new paradigm'.

eg → It is in this context that James and Prout (1997) critiqued the dominant framework and proposed their 'new paradigm' for researching children and childhood. The key aspects of this new approach were summarised in six points: ...

In each point, James and Prout critique what they see as the major weaknesses in the dominant framework. Childhood as a natural, biological phenomenon is contrasted with their view of childhood as a social construction. The universality

(Continued)

29

(Continued)

of childhood emphasised in developmental psychology and the socialisation perspective is replaced by recognition that childhoods are diverse. Research into children's relationships is given value and children are not seen in a vacuum. Children are recognised as social actors, actively constructing their own lives rather than as passive vessels to be filled with cultural awareness (Parsons 1956) and rational thought (Piaget 1955) ...

The new paradigm, the critique of the dominant framework, has also been subjected to critical analysis. Lee (2001) argues that by defining children as beings (in response to the dominant framework's focus on children as 'becomings' on a journey towards becoming fully human) the new paradigm is at odds with the ambiguity of modern childhood and indeed adulthood. ... In a later work, Prout (2005) notes that in focusing on childhood as a social construction, the new paradigm ignores the material components of social life ... In a similar vein, James and Prout (1997) admit that the relativism of the social constructionist approach cannot account adequately for the reality of 'political, social and economic maltreatment ventured against children on an international scale' (p. x) ...

Source: Fairbrother, 2010: 7–8

Theoretical underpinnings

In your literature review, it is important to introduce and discuss any theories and concepts which you intend to draw on to provide direction for your research and to help make sense of your data. Your own interpretation of these theories and concepts should be made clear. This could be done by first comparing and contrasting how others have debated and defined the theories and concepts, and then stating your own position.

The terms 'theory' and 'concept' tend to be interpreted and used in a variety of ways in different fields of research. However, generally speaking, a theory can be described as a framework which offers an explanatory device often in the form of categories and relationships. In the scientific sense, it is likely to be a proposition which both explains and predicts relationships between phenomena. In the social sciences this is not so clear-cut as human behaviour is less predictable and uniform than that of materials and substances.

A concept is a word or expression that represents a general or abstract idea which is derived from more specific instances; for example, 'democracy', 'social class' or 'stress'. In other words, a concept is a representation of an idea in a word or phrase. The use of concepts gives us a means of making sense of the world.

Example 2.7 Theoretical underpinnings

In the excerpt below Son introduces the theories of 'containment' and 'engagement' which provide a framework for his interpretation of relations between North and South Korea. He also relates the theories to the historical context of the research topic by referring to US policy after the cold war.

eg → The aim of this chapter is to provide an historical account of various strategies of containment and engagement and elucidate their theoretical grounding in order to uncover parallels and discrepancies between those strategies and identify the key conceptual components of comprehensive engagement, as proposed by this dissertation.

Containment is a by-product of the Cold War in which the United States and other Western states made all-out efforts to contain the ever-multiplying sphere of 'red' stretching across the Eurasian continent. In his seminal book, Strategies of Containment, Gaddis (1982) sought to analyse containment in terms of 'strategies' as a way to elucidate this illusive concept, which had undergone mutations and transformations through successive US administrations. As part of its global strategies of containment, the United States needed to build close alliances with democratic states worldwide, virtually establishing a wall around the Soviet Union and its allies and giving birth to such metaphors as Winston Churchill's 'Iron Curtain'. Even though the United States placed priority on rebuilding Western Europe, it also allocated limited resources to Asia. First, it turned to Japan in an attempt to find a key security partner in the region, while trying to make the war-devastated South Korea a frontline bulwark against communism (Iriye 1977; Ikenberry 2001a). In particular, the United States opened its market to Japanese and South Korean exports to help to reconstruct the two war-torn states, which could counterbalance the expansion of Communist states in East Asia. Nevertheless, the United States did not remain steadfast in its strategies of containment, as it deviated from its original roadmap to introduce strategies of limited engagement, as seen in the case of its engagement with China from the early 1970s onwards. This section will first offer an historical overview of strategies of containment and engagement, followed by a review of Cold War-related theories from the three perspectives of realism, liberalism and constructivism.

Source: Son, 2004: 14–15

Example 2.8 Theoretical underpinnings

In her literature review, Ling discusses four curriculum perspectives, three of which she draws on to provide a theoretical framework for her research. In the extract below, she introduces the liberal-progressive curriculum and contrasts it with the critical approach to the curriculum. In this part of her literature review, Ling relates each curriculum approach to the Chinese context and also to a range of Education for sustainable development curricula.

eg → Liberal-progressive sustainability education originated from the liberal-progressive curriculum perspective. Both the critical and liberal-progressive curriculum perspectives arose as a reaction against the technocratic and bureaucratic perspectives about and approaches to education in the West. Arising in the eighteenth century, however, the liberal-progressive curriculum perspective formed a distinctively different paradigm (Carr, 1998). While the critical curriculum perspective sees education as a socially transformative rather than socially reproductive agent, the liberal-progressive curriculum perspective sees education as being personal and intrinsically valuable in its own right, instead of as a means or agent for achieving certain goals (Peters, 1966). Inspired by the educational ideals espoused in Rousseau's *Émile* (Rousseau, 1762/1979), the liberal-progressive curriculum perspective focuses on 'rational autonomy and individual freedom' (Carr, 1998, p.327), supporting development of free thinking, responsible and morally mature individuals through personal fulfilment and comprehensive development of the mind, intelligence and imagination (Taylor and Richards, 1985). Liberal-progressive educators attach importance to the discovery and facilitation of learners' intuition from an early age, such as 'intuitive sense of justice' and 'innate child wisdom', throughout and beyond the years of formal education (Ashley, 2005, p.191).

Source: Feng, 2010: 44

Example 2.9 Theoretical underpinnings

In the example below, Hannah begins to draw out aspects from one paradigm for research with children that will underpin her own research. She starts off by recognising that the paradigm she is drawing on has itself been challenged (see Example 2.6 above) eg → Acknowledging these criticisms, some key concepts of the new paradigm are still useful in working out how to view children and engage in research with them. Matthews (2007) contests Thorne's assertion that the new paradigm has become 'middle aged' (Thorne 2006) and identifies three main ways in which it is still useful. First, it recognises children as playing a part in actively constructing their own lives. Second, there is an emphasis on exploring the plurality of childhoods, how different contexts affect children's relationships, rights and responsibilities. Third, the paradigm emphasises the relational structure of childhood and acknowledges that in these relationships adults have more power. Childhood, therefore, is to be understood as a minority category.

Source: Fairbrother, 2010: 7–8

Example 2.10 Theoretical underpinnings

The following extract introduces us to the theory of 'social constructionism', thus telling the reader about the theoretical perspective which informs the analysis of the social issue being investigated. The reader is informed about the philosophical origins of social constructionism, thereby situating the research historically in the field of sociological theory.

eg → An exploration of how social problems have been conceptualised reveals many broader trends within twentieth century sociology (Rubington and Weinberg 1995). Social constructionism has its philosophical roots in phenomenology (e.g. Schutz 1973; Berger and Luckmann 1966; Douglas 1970), ethnomethodology (e.g. Garfinkel 1973), and symbolic interactionism (e.g. Goffman 1959 and the works of Mead and Blumer). Together they call into question the taken-for-granted nature of reality and see the world as a product of human subjectivity: people define, interpret and give meaning to the world through their everyday actions and interactions.

Source: Calcraft, 2004: 19

Definitions and discussion of terminology used in the research

It is probable that you will use terminology in your research which has been defined and used in a variety of ways by different researchers in your field. This terminology is likely to encompass the labels given to concepts and theories, such as those mentioned in the section above, as well as more concrete nouns, such as 'social worker' or 'diabetes'. It is important that you do not assume a common agreement about the meaning of all the words and phrases that you include. You should therefore introduce your reader to the variety of ways a term has been defined and interpreted and/or make it clear how you will be using the term (see Chapter 8, Example 8.5).

Example 2.11 Definitions and discussion of terminology

Here the researcher discusses the terms 'diglossia' and 'polyglossia', providing relevant terminology and definitions for the research, and showing how different authors have used these terms in relation to particular social contexts.

eg → 'Diglossia' describes the linguistic situation where ... functional specialisation involves the appropriacy of using a particular language or variety, often referred to as the High (H) variety or less prestigious Low (L) variety. ... Nevertheless in many multilingual societies, the presence and use of intermediate varieties of languages reveal that the dichotomy between the H and L varieties may not exist as rigidly as in the classic diglossic situation just described. In view of this, Platt (1977) extends the term diglossia to polyglossia to refer to the linguistic situations in Singapore and Malaysia where several codes exist in a particular arrangement according to domains. In the same vein, Fasold (1984), taking examples from countries in Africa, emphasises that in multilingual language situations different forms of diglossia may exist, that is, there may be a High variety and several Low varieties existing alongside each other or different levels of H and L forms overlapping.

Source: Lee, 2003: 69

Example 2.12 Definitions of terminology

The researcher here clarifies the difference in meaning between conscious and unconscious goals for behaviour. Although citing definitions from other authors, the writer is also signalling that these are the definitions of the terms that he will be using for his research.

eg → When considering the influence of goals on behaviour it is useful to distinguish between conscious and unconscious goals. Conscious goals are those which are expressed in the form of a behavioural intention – instructions that people give to themselves to perform a certain behaviour (Triandis, 1980). Consequently, a conscious intention is the expression of an internal goal representation. In contrast, if the person is unaware that a goal is active, or unaware of its potential impact on behaviour, then the goal is deemed to be unconscious (Bargh, 1990; Bargh & Gollwitzer, 1994).

Source: Webb, 2003: 2

Signalling a gap in previous research and using this to justify your own

Example 2.13 The need for extension of previous work

It is a common feature of research generally to identify a 'gap' in previous research which your own work is well suited to fill. This general principle is illustrated in Moore's work, which signals the limitations and paucity of earlier research into the effectiveness of pronunciation instruction and shows how the current study is intended to fill the gap identified.

eg → Turning to research into pronunciation instruction and its effectiveness, the number of empirical studies is fewer and: 'Studies examining the effects of formal instruction in pronunciation have yielded inconsistent and even contradictory results.' (Elliott 1995: 531)

A study by Perlmutter (1989) found improved intelligibility on ESL learners during 6 months of instruction with particular emphasis on pronunciation. However, the subjects were all newcomers to the US and so could be expected to show significant improvement regardless of instruction. ... Further, instruction favouring prosodic features such as rhythm, intonation and stress seemed to enable students to transfer their learning to spontaneous situations whereas instruction with only segmental content did not produce such ability.

A study by Zborowska (1997, as discussed in Leather 1999) is reported as finding that explicit instruction helped both the learners' perceptual and productive acquisition of specific phonostylistic processes in comparison with a group which received no instruction.

(Continued)

35

(Continued)

In a study of the effects of different types of instruction (teacher correction, self-study in a language lab and interactive modification), McDonald et al. (op.cit. 94) reported 'that no single intervention was beneficial to all learners who experienced it. ...

The above studies provide us with neither a definitive answer to the question of whether pronunciation instruction does in fact help improve L2 proficiency, nor to which kind of instruction is most effective. ... However, more recent studies would seem to suggest that instruction may be beneficial with the importance of learner attitude and concern for pronunciation accuracy also being important factors in the process (Elliott op.cit.). Further studies into this area are needed to provide a stronger basis on which to plan a course of pronunciation. ...

The basic question under examination in this study is whether students who receive instruction in specific features of pronunciation perform better than those who do not.

Source: Moore, 2001: 7–17

The significance of a problem for research

In addition to indicating a gap in previous work, it is equally essential to underline the significance of the research you are proposing. A gap in previous research does not in itself provide justification for your own work. You should give good reasons why your study is important and worth doing. This might include a discussion of your motivation for doing the work; for instance in Example 2.13 the writer emphasised that her research was necessary to enable more effective course planning in the area of pronunciation instruction.

If outlining a problem that your research is intended to solve, it is advisable to incorporate citations from the literature in your field which support your claim that it should be investigated.

Example 2.14 Identifying
the problem to be investigated

Both a shortage of research in the area of sustainable urban drainage systems (SUDS) and the importance of conducting more research which assesses the level of pollutants in such systems are indicated here. The author provides supporting evidence of the need to investigate alternatives to traditional urban drainage systems – the overall problem – while also indicating a gap in knowledge about the way that SUDS operate.

eg → Many professionals are beginning to look towards sustainable urban drainage systems (SUDS) as an alternative to traditional urban drainage systems. SUDS attempt to store, treat and dispose of storm water closer to its source and are increasingly being viewed as effective measures to reduce run off volume, improve runoff quality and promote the recharging of groundwater (CIRIA 2000). Although SUDS have been incorporated into drainage designs for a number of years, they have failed to make a large-scale impact. Many believe this is due to the limited knowledge we have about their actual performance in the field (Delectic 1999) and the wide range of pollutant removals which are reported in various studies (Schueler et al. 1992; Young et al. 1996). It is now widely accepted that urban storm water is polluted and has detrimental effects on our waterways. However, few models exist at present which predict the movements of storm runoff and the pollutants held within it whilst travelling through a SUDS design. Such a model will help to assess the levels of pollutants being contained within SUDS and the levels that continue to reach our waterways.

Source: Overton, 2002: 1

Example 2.15 Identifying the problem and justifying the current research

Practical and theoretical reasons why the research is valuable are provided in this example. The researcher highlights the problem of employer–employee relations after radical organisational change and alludes to the scarcity of research in the area, thereby indicating a gap which the current study can fill.

eg → There is both practical and theoretical significance to a research study of this nature. The potential gains that can be realised if the employer–employee relationship is improved within the … Agency represents the practical significance of this study. … Very few organisations take the time to systematically review the state of their workforce in order to improve the employee–employer relationship, yet it is a key aspect of management training at the university and college level (Fry, Hattwick and Stoner 1998).

The theoretical significance of this study is that there has been very little organisational commitment research conducted in the public sector, let alone within an Agency

(Continued)

(Continued)

newly derived from the public sector. The results of this study will build upon the small amount of existing knowledge that helps public sector employers understand what reactions can be expected from employees following a radical structural and administrative change. These results will also facilitate knowledge-based recommendations that can be employed to better meet the expectations of the employees. To my knowledge, there has not been any published research within the field of organisational commitment that has been conducted within a government institution whose role involves a heritage conservation mandate. Therefore, ... this research will reveal organisational commitment results for an Agency ... that may differ from other public and private sector organizations. ... The more information collected and contributed to the organisational commitment body of literature, the better able managers will be to direct people in a way that best suits the objectives of both the organisation and the employee.

Source: Culverson, 2002: 22–4

Example 2.16 Linking the problem with a justification for the research focus

The justification for the research focus on higher education curricula in relation to sustainable development is given in the extract below. In the previous paragraph, Ling has identified the lack of comprehensive provision of education for sustainable development and here she justifies why she targets higher education institutions for her own research.

eg → HEIs have huge potential to play a significant role in contributing to sustainable development (SD) through sustainability education (Wang and Raninger, 2001; Gough and Scott, 2007). As many HEI graduates will move into responsible decision-making positions, it is important that they are able to make judgments and responsible decisions on various sides of SD issues as individuals and as members of society. Furthermore, as Corcoran et al. (2004) point out, HEIs can also benefit from introducing the notion of SD to HE, because sustainability education presents 'an opportunity to make education more problem based, more interdisciplinary and more applied' (p. 8).

Increasing numbers of HEIs have gradually realised their roles and responsibilities in contributing to sustainable development. The 1990s was a period when HEIs showed their commitments to SD intensively. The Talloires Declaration (1990), Halifax Declaration (1991), Swansea Declaration (1993) and Copernicus Charter (1993), which were all participated in by HEIs worldwide, confirmed their roles and responsibilities in education, research, operations, policy formation, networking and outreach in relation to SD. In terms of education, the Halifax Declaration encouraged HEIs to 'enhance the capacity of the university to teach and practise SD principles, to increase environmental literacy, and to enhance the understanding of environmental ethics among faculty, students and the public at large' (International Association of Universities, 1991, no page).

Source: Feng, 2010: 7

Task 2.1 Reflecting on your own research

Consider your own proposed research topic.

Using Table 2.1 as a template, consider and note down information which might be relevant for you to incorporate in your review, in relation to each of the suggested purposes of the literature review. In the third column note down the significant references you need to refer to in relation to each purpose. It is likely that you will gradually add to the third column (Key references) as your reading and research progresses.

For this task, think about the information that you want to include and not the order in which you will present it. How to develop your argument and an overall structure for your literature review will be considered in Chapter 6.

TABLE 2.1   The multiple purposes of your literature review

My research topic		
Research questions		
The purposes of the literature review	Relevant points to include in relation to your own research topic	Key references
Historical background		
Contemporary context		
Theories and concepts		
Relevant terminology		
Previous research and its limitations (the gap, the challenge, and/or extension)		
The significance of the issue being researched		
Other		

Summary

To summarise, this chapter has:

- discussed the multiple purposes which are likely to be realised in a literature review;
- looked at examples from dissertations and theses which illustrate the multiple purposes of a literature review in a range of different research contexts;
- provided a framework which can be used as a basis to explore your ideas about the relevant content for your own literature review.

3

Sources of information and conducting searches

Chapter summary

In this chapter, we are going to consider the importance of conducting a thorough and comprehensive literature search as part of the literature review process. More specifically, the chapter aims to:

- define the term 'literature search';
- discuss the reasons for carrying out a literature search;
- identify the different types of information sources which you are likely to access when involved in academic research;
- provide procedures for evaluating online sources;
- consider the variety of electronic tools you can use to search for information;
- outline an effective sequence of steps to take in the literature search process;
- illustrate the function of key words and Boolean logic when searching for information;
- introduce other electronic tools for supporting the literature search process such as RSS feeds and social bookmarking.

What is a literature search?

A literature search is defined by Sarah Gash (1999: 1) as 'a systematic and thorough search of all types of published literature in order to identify as many items as possible that are relevant to a particular topic'. It is a crucial part of the research process as it forms the basis of your reading and subsequently the written literature review which appears in your dissertation or thesis. It is an ongoing part of your work. In addition to doing a thorough literature search early on in the research process, it is important to continue to look for relevant reading throughout the project to ensure that nothing is missed and to keep up to date with new publications. It is also possible that the focus of your research may change during the course of your work, which makes it even more important to revisit and adapt your searches to cover this new direction in your thinking.

The availability of information electronically has meant that literature searching has become very much more complex than in the past, although the speed and convenience at which sources can be accessed has also increased. Not only is there a phenomenal amount of information available which you can retrieve from your own computer or mobile phone through the Internet, but also there is a wide variety of ways in which you can search for this information. The choices can be quite daunting when first starting on your research which is why most universities offer courses on information management. Doing a course such as this is time well spent and will help you to identify the most suitable search tools for your academic discipline and particular area of work. Even if you do not take a specific information management course, be sure to allow the library to be your friend and become comfortable about approaching the librarians for assistance. They will not be able to conduct your searches for you but they can offer guidance – and there may be subject specialists who can point you in the right direction for your research topic. Even if you are studying at a distance, there is likely to be a help desk you can phone or email for advice.

What are the purposes of a literature search?

In Chapter 2 we discussed the multiple purposes of the written literature review which appears in the thesis or dissertation, i.e. the literature review product. Now we turn to the purposes of the literature review process and, more specifically, the literature search.

There are a number of reasons why it is important to conduct a thorough literature search. In the first instance you need to identify the field and specific context in which your work is situated. At the beginning of your literature search your reading will be exploratory. You may have a hunch about something you wish to investigate but until you have read around the subject you may be uncertain about the focus and therefore the exact background in which you wish to place your work. Your literature search can give you ideas about the focal point of your research and the wider context in which it will sit. As well as helping you home in on a topic, it can assist you in identifying your approach to the research and the methodology you wish to adopt. More specifically, it will help you identify the type of data you might collect and use, sites of data collection, the sample size and how you might analyse this data.

In addition to reading around the topic as a means of identifying what and how you wish to research, it is essential that you gain a thorough and comprehensive knowledge of the field. Your literature search and the reading are a means of extending your understanding of the key concepts, theories and methodologies in the field. By increasing your awareness, knowledge and understanding of the area, you will be in a better position to make informed choices about the important research related issues identified above.

Another important reason for a rigorous literature search is to find out what others have done in the area so as to avoid duplicating previous work. This enables you to ensure the originality of your work – an essential prerequisite for PhD research. By exploring previous research in the field, you can identify areas where research has not yet been undertaken, how the work of others could be extended, how questions which previous research has left unanswered can be addressed, and how to avoid repeating mistakes that others have made. In other words, you can identify the gap or niche (Swales, 1990) that your research can fill.

A further purpose of your literature search is to identify key people, organisations and texts which are relevant to your research. Relevant organisations might include academic, government and professional bodies. There will be key journals in your field in which peer-reviewed articles are published. You should identify which journals are relevant for you and keep referring to them on a regular basis throughout your research for significant publications. As you continue to trawl through the literature you will begin to notice familiar names and hence identify key researchers in your area of interest. You may find it useful to search for all their published work and keep an eye on their current publications.

It is clear a range of purposes is served by searching the literature. As stated above, it is crucial to include literature searching as an ongoing part of the research process, although your purposes will shift from being exploratory to becoming more focused as your reading progresses.

Sources of information

In this section, we consider the different information sources that are available. When conducting academic research you will not be restricted to one particular type of publication or information source but will want to investigate the full range of relevant materials. The most common sources are summarised below.

Books

Books are likely to be the first port of call for many new researchers as a means of beginning the exploratory journey in and around the field. Your university library bookshelves are lined with books in printed form and, increasingly, it is possible to access many of them electronically as ebooks. It is now possible to read many books on a portable ebook reader, such as a Kindle, the device produced by the international online retailer, Amazon. Whether accessed in printed or electronic form, there is a variety of types of book you may refer to as part of your work. The following are the most important.

Textbooks contain the underpinning principles, concepts and theories of a field. They often contain information which is generally accepted as being commonly agreed knowledge in a field.

Specialised books may for example report on research completed for a PhD thesis or a specific theoretical area of a field of research. They may include a collection of chapters written by different authors on a particular specialist theme with an overall editor or editorial board that has collected together and reviewed the contributions for the book. For example, papers from a conference may be published as conference proceedings.

Reference books such as dictionaries, encyclopaedias, directories are used to find specific information or definitions. These are now likely to be available in electronic and/or printed format. Electronic versions are often accessible both online and on CD ROM.

Journal articles

Journals contain collections of peer-reviewed academic articles which are written by different researchers or practitioners in a particular field. Each journal has a specific set of purposes and an intended audience, all of which are usually articulated in each issue that is published. The peer review process means that other academics or professionals in the field have reviewed and made recommendations about each article published, therefore ensuring its quality. Journals include the most recent ideas in circulation in a discipline and the majority are now available electronically.

University libraries subscribe to a large number of journals both in printed and electronic format; however, after conducting your literature search you may wish to access an article in a journal to which your library does not subscribe. It is usually possible to access the article through an interlibrary loan from a central location such as the British Library. It is also worth doing a search for the article using Google Scholar although you may well find that it is not available free of charge if accessed in this way.

Most journals publish between three and six issues in a single year; the issues in one year are collated into a volume. So, for example, you might see the following reference:

Higher Education 20/3: 260–83.

Name of journal Volume/Issue: page numbers.

Published literature reviews of a field

These may be in the form of either a journal article or a book and provide a summary and synthesis of research and/or theory in a field. They are known as systematic reviews and are usually undertaken by a team of academics and professionals to investigate a clearly focused aim or question. Organisations, such as the Cochrane Collaboration in the healthcare field, provide a collection of systematic reviews to inform practice. A published literature review provides a useful introduction and overview of a field, but it is important not to rely solely on these as, when doing your thesis or dissertation literature review, you should demonstrate that you are able to identify and interpret the relevant original sources yourself (see Chapter 11 for more on systematic literature reviews).

'Grey literature'

Other important sources of information are gathered under the umbrella term of 'grey literature'. The term refers to material that is not published commercially and is difficult to obtain through the usual book-selling and bibliographical channels. Typically, grey literature includes: reports, theses and dissertations, conference proceedings, research in progress, leaflets and posters, media reports, patents, letters, and diaries.

Reports Could be written by companies or government organisations and might report, for example, on an investigation into an event or situation, its findings and recommendations.

Theses and dissertations It can be helpful to access the research of other masters and doctoral students by reading their theses and dissertations. Electronic versions are becoming more widely available; for example, EthOS is the British Library's Electronic Thesis Online Service, through which an increasing number of UK PhD theses can be accessed. Otherwise, hard copies of theses and dissertations need to be requested from the library where they are held through the interlibrary loan facility or from a country's central library (e.g. the British Library) in printed form or as a CD/DVD. Some theses and dissertations may have been published in a more concise form as either a book or a selection of journal articles.

Conference literature Academic conferences produce collections of printed abstracts and often published proceedings. Proceedings consist of a selection of the papers presented at the conference.

Popular media Newspapers, practitioner trade journals and magazines may be relevant for some research topics so that a researcher can find out about contemporary events and interpretations, and reactions from the general public.

Monographs/work-in-progress papers Some research centres may make specialist papers available which are produced for other researchers and professionals in the field.

Specialist literature and primary data sources In some specialist fields, the literature may also include maps, music, diaries, letters, manuscripts of poems and novels, patents and other legal documents.

Web sites

A range of different types of information can be found through web sites and judgments about the quality of the material accessed have to be made on an individual basis. Some examples of the types of web sites that could be used as sources of information are mentioned here.

Professional organisations such as the British Psychological Association (http://www.bps.org.uk/) can provide a wealth of information on publications, conferences and relevant press releases. UK government sites such as that of the Department for Education (http://www.education.gov.uk/) provide access to policy documents, reports and resources. Charities such as Oxfam (http://www.oxfam.org.uk/) give information about world events and appeals and access to development reports and resources. Increasingly, sites such as these incorporate the use of social media such as Flickr, Twitter, Facebook, blogs, podcasts and YouTube videos, all of which are useful for gaining up-to-date information about the current debates and issues in an area of practice.

Wikipedia (http://en.wikipedia.org/wiki/Main_Page) is an online encyclopaedia which anyone can edit. It is not usually deemed to be an academically reliable source of information but it can, however, provide an overview of a field which must then be explored further through other more rigorously reviewed sources of information. If using a Wikipedia entry to provide you with information, it is essential to evaluate the references cited and access these to evaluate and use for your own work. Many academic institutions do not accept Wikipedia as a reference in your bibliography due to the open access editing of its pages.

Individual academics usually have their own web pages with their professional details and interests as well as lists of their publications. If you have identified a particular author as key for your research, accessing their personal web page can take you to recent publications which may be important for your work.

Evaluating online sources of information

All sources of information should be evaluated carefully before including in your academic writing and it is especially the case for online resources. This is because anybody can put information on the Internet and the material is not necessarily subject to peer-review quality checks. For a list of references in your academic writing, you should be able to include both the author and date for every source; if either is not traceable it is important to consider carefully whether the reference should be used. As a web site does not always display this information clearly, the points that follow should be addressed to assess its suitability as a source to cite in your work.

- Analyse the URL (Uniform Resource Locator) address to assess the site's credibility: the URL address is the address that you see in the browser at the top of the screen when viewing a web site and the suffixes that appear after the organisation name give you important information. The examples below are home pages of a selection of web sites from different organisation types.

.ac and .edu = educational institutions (http://www.shef.ac.uk/)

.org = non governmental and non-profit making organisation
(http://www.farmafrica.org.uk/)

.gov = government organisation   (http://www.dft.gov.uk/)

.co and .com = commercial organisation (http://www.canon.co.uk/)

The country code (e.g. .uk for the United Kingdom or .my for Malaysia) tells you the country of origin of the site.   (http://www.tourismconcern.org.uk/)
(http://www.tourism.gov.my/)

When exploring information on the Internet and moving between web sites, a hyperlink from one web site may take you to any page within another site; it is important to click on the home page tab at the top of a web page to orient yourself in relation to the material. Understanding the URL structure of a web site is also helpful and often there is a 'site map' tab which will show you the structure of the entire site and enable you to find your way more quickly to the information that you need.

- Who or what organisation has produced the site? Do you already know that this author or organisation has an established reputation in your field? If the author is anonymous, it is advisable not to use the site for an academic reference as you have no way of assessing its credibility. If, on the other hand, you can identify the author or organisation but you do not already recognise them as a reliable source, you should make some further investigations to establish whether they are credible in the field. For example, there may have been a link to this site from a source that you trust. The site may have an 'About us' tab from which you can discover more. You can find out about an author's professional background and qualifications by doing an Internet search for the author or organisation name. Search for other publications by this author in library catalogues and bibliographical databases. All of these techniques can help you establish whether the author or organisation is recognised and established in the field.
- When was the site produced or last edited? Can you find a publication date or a 'last updated' entry on the site. Explore the tabs at the top of the site for this information (e.g. there may be an 'About' tab) or look at the bottom of the page. Again, if you do not know when the information was written, it may not be suitable to use. If a publication date is given but the source is old, assess whether this makes it unsuitable for your purpose.
- What type of online resource is it? If you have accessed a form of social media such as a wiki or blog it will not have been peer reviewed and therefore may not be suitable to cite in an academic paper. The use of information from a social media source may be acceptable in certain disciplines and contexts but this should be confirmed with tutors.
- Is the content presented in a logical way with strong enough evidence? Does the author appear to be presenting a balanced argument? Is there a list of references included and do you recognise them as being credible in your field? If there are errors in grammar, punctuation and spelling, it is likely that the source has not been peer reviewed or even checked and hence is not a reputable source to use. The guidance given on critical reading in Chapters 4 and 8 is also applicable when evaluating online sources of information.

Different types of research

Some of the specialist literature accessed may well be the data or the object of study. Research which uses literature as the data for the study is often referred to as 'armchair' or 'library-based' research and is common in fields such as law, history and literature.

Briefly to clarify this distinction in the way the literature may be used, it is helpful to differentiate between two types of research. For many researchers, their data come from conducting interviews, doing experiments, observing behaviour, etc. The focus is on collecting information that has not been recorded before. This can be referred to as empirical research, where the researcher is actively going out into the field or working in the laboratory to explore and to discover new information. An alternative kind of research occurs when the data set consists of documents or texts. In this second scenario, the literature itself provides the source of data and therefore is the focus of analysis. Of course, there are some research projects which combine both empirical and library-based research. For example, a researcher investigating patent law might combine both an analysis of the relevant legal documents with interviews with legal practitioners who interpret the laws and regulations.

Tools for finding relevant sources

As stated, many of the information sources you require may be available in electronic form; for example, an increasing number of journals are avail-able electronically through your library web page or open access networks (e.g. Directory of Open Access Journals – DOAJ (http://www.doaj.org/). There may be links to a journal article or electronic version of a book from an indi-vidual academic's personal web page.

Having summarised the main types of information sources that you are likely to consult, in this section we move on to consider the main tools you can use to initiate your searches for this information. It is important to spend some time becoming aware of and familiar with the search options available to you as the efficient use of these tools is an essential part of the research process. Broadly speaking, the search tools available can be divided into the following categories:

- catalogues;
- bibliographical databases;
- Internet search engines;
- open access databases;
- professional organisation web sites;

In what follows I describe each one of these and give some examples. To help you identify the most suitable databases and gateways to use in your subject area, you can try an alphabetical search for the relevant subject area on your library web page and/or consult your supervisor and colleagues in your department.

Catalogues

Library catalogues (Online Public Access Catalogues – OPACs) Library catalogues or OPACs provide the bibliographical details and locations of all the publications held within a particular library. Most UK libraries use Dewey Decimal Classification and in the USA the majority employ the Library of Congress Classification. In both systems, books are categorised according to subject with specific shelf numbers allocated.

The catalogue is likely to be a computer database which can be accessed on the university network. Hence, if you have access to a university computer or an Internet connection you do not actually have to be in the library to use it for your searches. Most operate in a similar way, allowing you to conduct key word searches by subject, author or title. It is a good idea to spend some time becoming familiar with how to carry out efficient searches in your library catalogue in order that you make use of its full potential. Ask a librarian for advice if you need to.

Copac National, Academic and Specialist Library Catalogue This is the combined online catalogue of an increasing number of research universities in the UK and Ireland, including the British Library and the National Library of Scotland and the National Library of Wales. It is a freely available catalogue that enables you to conduct wider searches than possible on an individual university library catalogue and locate where resources are held. More libraries, including some specialist libraries and collections are being added all the time. The Copac web page provides up-to-date information on the catalogue; see http://www.copac.ac.uk/.

National catalogues Many countries have their own national catalogues which list all the publications available in the country. Two examples are:

- British Library Integrated Catalogue. This catalogue operates from the British Library, which has a copy of all the publications available in the UK. It can be accessed from the following web page: http://www.bl.uk/catalogues/listings.html. Zetoc (http://zetoc.mimas.ac.uk/index.html) is the British Library's electronic table of contents for a large number of current journals and conference proceedings dating from 1993. Links are provided to aid access to the full texts of these articles and papers. The resource is freely available to members of subscribing educational institutions and the National Health Service in England, Scotland and Northern Ireland. Email alerts and RSS feeds can be set up so that you receive up-to-date information when new articles and journals are added to the database.
- Library of Congress catalog for the US. From this home page you can conduct searches on the Library of Congress catalogue and access catalogues from many other libraries in the world: http://www.loc.gov/z3950/.

BUBL Link BUBL Link is a catalogue of Internet resources. It provides a link to OPACs of other universities around the world as well as to many other Internet resources. You are likely to be able to access this link from your university library web page on: http://www.bubl.ac.uk/ link/types/opacs.htm.

Publishers' and booksellers' catalogues Booksellers such as Amazon (http://www. amazon.co.uk) and publishers such as Sage (http://www.sage. co.uk/) have catalogues which provide lists of all books published. Searches can be made by subject, author and key word. This can be a useful way of searching for the most recently published books in a field.

Bibliographical databases

University libraries have subscriptions to a multitude of different electronic databases and electronic journals. You usually need university username and password details to access these.

A bibliographical database is an organised list of publications in a particular subject area. The publications included vary between different databases but their main focus is usually on journal articles and conference papers. Bibliographical databases of systematic literature reviews are also becoming an increasingly important source of information. On your university library web pages, it will be possible to search for relevant databases for your subject area and generally speaking you will be able to find a description of each one either on the library web page or when you first access the database. When you identify relevant publications on a database, you will retrieve enough information to then be able to find the publication in a library or through electronic means. In many cases, an abstract will also be provided which gives a summary of the work and you will be able to link to an electronic version of the full text. It is important to note that you are more likely to be able to access the full text of journal articles if conducting your searches when logged on through your university account with a personal username and password than if using an open access search route such as Google Scholar. This is because access may depend on your university subscription to the electronic journal concerned.

Originally databases such as these were available in printed form and, depending on your research, you may still need to consult printed collections of abstracts and indexes if searching for older sources. But electronic databases are now the norm either through networked computer services or on CD ROM.

Some examples of databases include: the Web of Knowledge (WoK) for literature in the sciences, social sciences, arts and humanities; MEDLINE for biomedical literature; ProQuest for ebooks, journal articles and dissertations in a wide range of disciplines; the Cochrane database of systematic reviews in the area of health; Index to theses (UK theses); EthOS (the British Library's Electronic Thesis Online Service); and Dissertation abstracts (US and worldwide dissertations and theses). As mentioned, by logging in as a user to your library web page, you will find the range of databases available which relate to your subject area.

As an individual database may not scan all the journals which may be of interest, it is important to consult more than one database in your field. And because different databases tend to vary with their rules for searches and their use of Boolean operators, it is advisable to use the help menu on an individual database to get tips on efficient approaches to adopt when devising key word combinations.

Internet search engines

Search engines are very large databases. They trawl a large number of other databases and web sites to look for information to create their own database of web pages. Search engines are created by robots which crawl through numerous web pages and add them to the database according to the presence of key words within the web documents. Within a particular search engine, you can look for information by entering key words in the 'search' box. A series of web documents is then retrieved. The most popular and plausible results usually appear first on the list and you can select the ones that look most relevant for your purposes. Two of the most widely known search engines are: Google – http://www.google.com/ and Altavista – http://www.altavista.com/.

Different search engines collect information in slightly different ways, so it is a good idea to become familiar with more than one. You can see the variation by trying out the same key word searches in two or more search engines and comparing the results. Use the site-specific help menu and advanced search option on each one to help you develop efficient searching techniques.

As a word of caution and as discussed above, Internet references are not reliable academic sources if you are unable to trace who produced the material and if the purpose of the documentation is not clear. It is therefore important to use web-based information cautiously and evaluate it carefully before citing it in your academic writing.

Google scholar Google scholar (http://scholar.google.com/) is a more specific search engine which, as the name suggests, provides a tool to search for scholarly or academic web page links. You can search by key word/s or author and find an extensive range of peer-reviewed articles, books, reports and information about the number of times and where these items are cited in other publications. Google scholar also provides information on where and how you can obtain the texts you are looking for.

Open access databases: the Open Archive Initiative

A number of open access repositories of information are now available on the Internet. This means that access to the documents included in a database is available to all and is not dependent on an individual or institution subscription. Two examples are given below:

- Directory of Open Access Journals (DOAJ). This is a database of open access journals from a range of different subject areas. An increasing number of journals are being added to this directory. A user can gain access to the full text of many of the articles in the journals which are listed. The DOAJ is available on http://www.doaj.org/.
- PubMed. This is a publicly available version of Medline which provides information in the field of health and medical sciences. It is made available by the US National Library of Medicine, on http://www.ncbi.nlm.nih.gov/pubmed/.

Professional organisations As mentioned above, there are many professional organisations with web sites which provide a large quantity of useful information, contacts and links which can lead you to relevant and up-to-date sources. For example, the United Kingdom Literacy Association (UKLA) (http://www.ukla.org/) is a registered charity which promotes effective practice in literacy education in a wide range of settings. It includes links to journals, publishers and resources and provides information about contemporary debates and conferences. Through professional organisation web sites such as these, it is possible to discover the key authors for your field of research, thus helping to ensure you have identified all the significant literature.

Some examples from other fields include the Royal College of Nursing (RCN) (http://www.rcn.org.uk/), the Chartered Institute of Public Finance and Accountancy (CIPFA) (http://www.cipfa.org.uk/), the Law Society (http://www.lawsociety.org.uk/home.law) and The Institution of Engineering and Technology (IET) (http://www.theiet.org/). To find out which professional organisations might be important for your research, conduct a key word search for 'professional organisations *your subject area*' on your Internet browser.

The process of conducting a literature search

In this part of the chapter, the actual process of doing a literature search is considered. In the above section, the focus was on the electronic possibilities for ensuring your search is comprehensive and complete. In what follows, when considering the overall process, I emphasise the importance of spending real time in the library alongside your electronic searches, and the value and role of the snowball technique when you follow up references from the bibliographies of books and articles that you read. Serendipity, the fortuitous and unexpected discovery of something useful, is another important aspect of literature searching. You may find a key source when browsing along the shelves in the library, when chatting to a colleague at a conference or after clicking on a different tag on a social bookmarking site.

Get to know the library

Although more and more information is available electronically, the libraries and their printed resources must not be forgotten. Despite the convenience of being able to access the literature you need from your desk or even your mobile phone, you may still enjoy browsing the shelves and looking at the printed volumes. It is a good idea to start your literature search with a visit to your university library. If you are following a distance-learning course, this is more difficult to do but if at all possible it is helpful to have access to a comprehensive university library throughout your research. Go on an organised library tour if possible to find out the details of where different types of information are stored and to familiarise yourself with the systems for the various facilities you may wish to use. For example, if you are investigating a fairly specific and unusual issue, you may need to read documents which are not in your own university library. To access them you will probably have to make use of the interlibrary loan facility and order books or copies of articles from a central resource, such as the British Library Document Supply Centre. Therefore, it is useful to discover whether and/or how you can make use of this system in your particular university library.

Find the shelves in your university library which have the books most closely connected to the topic you wish to research. A general key word search for your subject in the library catalogue will direct you to the shelves you need. Books will help give you an overview and broad understanding of the field, and help you to identify a more specific topic and key words for more detailed and refined searches. Of course, all the books you need may not be in the same location – especially if you are making novel connections between different disciplines. Also remember that libraries usually have separate shelf sequences and locations for oversized books. Once you have identified the various relevant physical locations of books related to your topic, return regularly and browse along these shelves as you may come across unexpected titles that could be useful. At different points in your research, you will have varying priorities in your mind and different titles may strike you as being important at different times. Electronic books or ebooks are widely available through university libraries now, so also make full use of the online catalogue to find out which ones your library stocks and how to access them.

In a similar way, become familiar with where the journals are shelved. Identify the journals which you think are likely to be most relevant for you and look at the new issues regularly. Journal articles cited in books will help lead you to the key journals in your field. You can also identify relevant journal articles electronically through key word searches of bibliographical databases. Most journals are now available online so it is possible to download articles onto your own computer. Furthermore, in recent years, there has been a proliferation of journals which are *only* available electronically. Email alerts and RSS feeds (see section below) are widely available tools that can be incorporated into your research activities to ensure that you receive notification of updates to web sites and new publications of relevance.

To take advantage of the electronic search facilities now available, familiarise yourself with your university library web pages, which you will be able to access from your university web site. As you explore these pages, you will find they offer a wealth of resources and advice as well as access to catalogues and links that will take you all over the world searching for information (in the virtual sense, of course). If you are studying at a distance, the online potential of libraries will offer you the means to do much of your literature searching from your own computer or other mobile device with Internet access. To access the electronic possibilities of literature searching, you will need the following: a personal computer with a modem; a telephone connection, if possible with broadband and a WiFi connection; an Internet Service Provider (ISP) such as Tiscali; and browser software such as Internet Explorer. Increasingly, smart phones such as BlackBerrys and iPhones are also being used for Internet browsing although the small size of their screens is a disadvantage.

Consult colleagues and your supervisor

Consult your supervisor and colleagues for references that will introduce you to the field but do your own searches as well. Your supervisor may be happy to advise you on the most useful electronic databases to use for your literature searches but he or she may, equally, deliberately leave this for you to discover for yourself. Part of the challenge of doing research is to be independent and this includes making your own decisions about how and where to search for information and what to read. If, however, you feel uncertain about what you are doing and begin to feel lost or overwhelmed, ask your supervisor or a librarian for help.

Some journals publish review articles which give a synthesis of research and theory in a particular area in the form of systematic literature reviews. If you find one relevant to your topic it provides a good resource but it is important to have a look at the original articles yourself as well. Your supervisor may be able to direct you to such an integrative review if there is a relevant and recent one which relates to your intended topic.

Key word searches

When you have a more detailed idea about the topic you wish to research, you can start to identify your key words and conduct searches on the library catalogue

(OPAC), wider catalogues such as Copac or BUBL, electronic databases, and search engines. The identification of key words involves the selection of nouns and adjectives which most accurately describe the content that you are looking for. When devising your key words, it may be helpful to consult dictionaries, thesauri and encyclopaedias to consider all the alternative words and spellings that cover your topic of interest.

Use the key words specified in articles you read to help you devise further key word searches for yourself. But be aware that even when using key words you may miss articles. The authors of a particular article may have chosen key words to describe their work that are different from the ones you have selected for your search, even though the article may be on the theme that you are looking for. It is therefore important to try out a number of different key word alternatives and combinations.

Keep a record of all your key word searches and where you conduct each one to avoid repeating the same searches at a later date. The systems you can use for organising your searches and reading are discussed in Chapter 5, while Chapter 4 discusses how to cope with the quantity of reading and how to be selective about which texts you actually access from your searches. In the section below on social bookmarking, I explain how tagging is an important development which relates to the use of key words.

The snowball technique

As you read around the subject, you are likely to redefine the focus of your research, which may lead to new or revised key word searches. You will begin to recognise familiar authors and cited texts in the bibliographies of the books and articles that you are reading, and will therefore start to look for more specific texts in catalogues and journals. The snowball technique, when you follow up references from the bibliographies of the texts you read, is well used. In the most obvious sense, this involves following up references to previous work but many electronic databases and journals now allow you to track forward citations. If, for example, you are looking at an article published in 2004, you can find the articles published subsequently in which the 2004 article has been cited. In my experience, extending the scope of your reading by the snowball technique tends to be more common than key word searches as the research becomes more focused and the researcher becomes more familiar with the literature in the field.

As the literature search is a process that will go on for the entire period of your research it is important to keep a record of the steps that you work through. Table 3.1 below as part of Task 3.1 is suggested as a useful checklist for you to follow.

The use of key words and Boolean logic

This section of the chapter includes some general guidance on the use of key words. It is possible to make your key words searches more sophisticated by using Boolean logic. This system is named after the English mathematician George Boole (1815–64). It describes the system of symbols and words that can be used to conduct searches by combining key words into search statements. These search statements allow you to be quite specific about the information you are looking for by indicating what you want included and excluded in your search. Different catalogues, databases and search engines have slight variations in the way they use Boolean logic operators so it is worth checking on their help menus or advanced search options for details.

The basic principles of three of the most useful logical operators – AND, OR, and wildcards – are described here. By combining words with AND, a search will be made for documents that contain both these words. Sources that include only one of these words will be ignored. For example, if you enter obesity AND teenagers, the documents retrieved will contain both the words obesity and teenagers. Similarly, by combining words with OR, a search will be made for documents which contain either of these words. The use of OR is helpful when there are two very similar terms and you wish to broaden the search to find texts which use either word: for example, youth OR teenagers. In this case, the documents retrieved will contain either the word youth or the word teenagers.

The third option is to use a wildcard symbol such as an asterisk – *. The wildcard symbol replaces a character or characters in a word. It can be used with a root word so that all variations of the word will be searched for, or within a word so that alternative spellings will be included. Wildcard symbols vary, so check in the relevant help menu to confirm which you should use on a particular database or search engine. Examples using an asterisk wildcard include:

- col*r – allows for different spellings of colour;
- migrat* – allows for different variations which derive from the root: migrate, migrated, migrating, migration.

As noted above, you will be able to conduct the most efficient searches by looking at the advanced search or help menus on the catalogues, databases, subject gateways and search engines you are using. They offer you different ways of inputting your key word searches. For example, if doing an advanced search using the search engines Google or Google Scholar, the AND, OR, and NOT functions appear using the following wording: Find articles with *all* the words; with the *exact phrase*; with *at least one* of the words; *without* the words (see Screenshot 3.1).

SCREENSHOT 3.1   Google Scholar (c) Google Inc. Used with permission.

In essence, there are two aspects of key word searching which are important:

- the identification of all the key words which accurately and succinctly describe what you are looking for;
- the use of these key words and logical operators efficiently in the various catalogues and databases that you employ for your searches.

Keeping up to date: RSS feeds and email alerts

RSS (Really Simple Syndication) feeds or news feeds are a means of channelling new information from selected web pages to a personal news reader or to the 'favourites' collection on your own computer. By setting up RSS feeds, the latest information comes to one location rather than you having to access each journal, web page, blog, etc., individually to find out whether any new information has become available. An RSS feed can be set up from any online location that displays the RSS symbol 🔝. You will need to subscribe to the feed on each web page from which you would like to receive updates by clicking on this symbol and following the instructions. Although you can add RSS feeds to the 'favourites' list on your own computer, you are also likely to need a personal newsfeed reader such as Google reader, especially if you like to access updates from different computers and/or your mobile phone. The news reader constantly checks your selected news sites, databases, blogs and journals for new content and 'feeds' this to your reader. RSS feeds are a helpful method for receiving the most recent information and this is valuable for ensuring that your literature review is current. The downside is the possibility of an overload of information. Hence, RSS feeds should be set up carefully and each one should be scrutinised to assess its relevance for your topic area.

Another technique for receiving updates involves email alerts. You can register to receive email alerts from some publishers' web pages, journals and databases to match the search criteria that you specify. These alerts will arrive in your email inbox.

Social bookmarking

One further tool for literature searching and also for sharing sources with others who have related interests is a social bookmarking site such as CiteULike (http://www.citeulike.org/). Sites such as this one offer a very different way of finding, accessing, recording and retrieving information and also a way of creating and extending research communities so that the process of collecting relevant literature is not such an isolated activity.

Social bookmarking sites have developed from the commonly used bookmarking facility through which we can add useful web sites to the 'favourites' menu on our web browser tool bar. This enables us to access a web site at a later date with a single click on the 'favourite' link we have created. The limitation of traditional bookmarking is that it is tied to a specific computer and often to an individual user. With social bookmarking, your bookmark is placed on a web site which is accessible from multiple locations and is available to other interested participants.

To use social bookmarking to assist in the literature search process, you first need to select a social bookmarking site such as CiteULike; this particular site has been available since 2004 and is specifically designed for researchers to find, store and share electronically available research papers for their field. After joining the site, links to articles of interest can be saved to a personal library. On CiteULike, bibliographical details are added automatically and personal 'tags' or key words can be created for categorisation purposes. Comments and ratings can be made about the papers added.

In terms of searching for literature, 'tagging' is essential as a user can search for all articles with a particular tag, thus finding other related papers and connecting with others with similar interests who have used the same tags. It is possible to see who else has bookmarked the same article and access their libraries to identify other papers.

There are some additional features of CiteULike which can assist in literature searching. First, RSS feeds can be set up so that you receive notification of new postings and second, bibliographical links can be exported to reference management software such as EndNote (see Chapter 5). Privacy settings are also available and tag clouds show the most commonly used tags in a larger font than those less frequently used.

There are, however, some potential disadvantages to the use of a social bookmarking tool. There is no monitoring of 'tagging' so accuracy and appropriacy are dependent on responsible and careful use by the participants on a site. In addition, a personal library on a social bookmarking site could become yet one more online location to monitor and update. Thus, for your own research, you must make choices about which resources suit your own purposes and preferences best. Social bookmarking offers the potential of an online research community which may or may not suit your own needs and research context.

Task 3.1 Tracking and recording your search

The checklist template provided in Table 3.1 will enable you to track and record your literature search. In particular, it is important to keep a clear record of which key word searches you have conducted and in which catalogues, databases, subject gateways and search engines. As noted, completing the checklist is an ongoing task. If you are in the early stages of your research, it is important to familiarise yourself with the type of record you will need to keep. If you have already started your literature searches, make sure you have adopted a comprehensive record-keeping system, such as indicated in Table 3.1.

Think of a key word search that you wish to do in relation to your topic, e.g. recycling AND urban OR city OR municipal.

Try your key word search in your library catalogue, an electronic database for your subject area, and an Internet search engine such as Google Scholar. Make a record of all the useful 'hits' on Table 3.1 and compare your results for each search.

TABLE 3.1   A record of your literature search – a checklist

The proposed topic of my research			
Key word searches have been completed in the following places:			
Name of catalogue, database, search engine or social bookmarking site	Key word searches conducted or tags used	Results of search (e.g. articles and books located)	Date of search

The shelf numbers where I am likely to find books relevant for my research:

Some key books which I have identified for my research:

A useful integrative review of previous work in my field:

Key journals which I have identified for my research:

Important authors/researchers in my field:

Useful professional web sites:

Social bookmarking sites/groups:

Blogs/wikis:

 Summary

To summarise, this chapter has:

- defined the term 'literature search';
- explored the reasons why a rigorous literature search is important for research;
- considered the different types of information sources that can be consulted;
- summarised points to take into account when evaluating web sites and online resources;
- examined the various electronic tools available for conducting searches;
- outlined a process to work through when conducting a literature search;
- looked at key words and Boolean operators;
- described the purpose of RSS feeds and email alerts;
- outlined the potential of social bookmarking sites;
- provided a checklist to assist you in keeping track of your literature search.

4

Reading and note-taking strategies

Chapter summary

This chapter overviews effective approaches to reading and note taking, more specifically looking at.

- the reasons for reading;
- techniques for efficient reading;
- the adoption of a critical, analytical and evaluative approach to texts;
- strategies for note taking;
- techniques for writing an effective summary;
- ways of observing and noting connections between different source texts.

In particular, the chapter aims to emphasise the need to be a critical reader: reading actively and analytically, making connections with what you already know and evaluating the strengths and weaknesses of an author's research and arguments (also see Chapter 8, on critical writing).

Let us first of all consider the reasons why reading is such an important part of the research process. We have identified some of the reasons already when thinking about the purposes of a literature search in Chapter 3. Incorporating and expanding on these, we can say that reading contributes to the research process and helps you to:

- find out more about the field in which you are working and identify a topic for the research;
- develop your own understanding of the field;
- find out what other research has been done in the area;
- keep up to date with developments in the field;
- place your own research in a context;
- identify theoretical perspectives that you might wish to draw on;
- find support for your views and arguments;
- explore possible research methods to use for your own research;
- pursue your enjoyment of reading around the subject;
- explore different perspectives in the field and position yourself among them;
- make observations about writing conventions in your discipline to develop your own academic writing style.

At first, it is not unusual to feel overwhelmed by the quantity and variety of literature available. However, as your research topic becomes more fine-tuned, you will gradually become more able to recognise the texts that are most relevant to you and hence the material that you need to read thoroughly and in detail. An important way to cope with the large quantity of reading is to adopt efficient approaches and techniques, first in the selection of the most relevant material to read and, second, when actually reading these texts in detail. If you have a clearly defined purpose in your mind when you read a text, it will help you adopt the most appropriate strategies for the circumstances.

At different stages in the research process, we read for different reasons. In the first instance, our reading is *exploratory*; we want to find out more about the topic and explore ideas in a fairly free-ranging way. Later, we have to adopt a more *focused* approach when more precise research questions have been formulated. At this point, you read for more specific information, such as to find evidence and authority to back up your assertions, contrasting definitions on a particular concept you are using, or reasons for the choice of a particular research method. In fact, not only do we read in different ways depending on our purpose at a particular point in time but also it is common to revisit key sources of information as you will find you take different things from a text according to your focus at a specific moment in the research process.

Techniques for reading efficiently

SQ3R

A commonly recommended procedure for reading efficiently is known as SQ3R (Survey, Question, Read, Recall, Review). By following the suggested steps, you are actively encouraged to interact with the text instead of taking in the information in a passive and unquestioning way (see Box 4.1). It is, of course, a strategy which can be used flexibly according to your individual preference and purpose for reading at a particular time.

Box 4.1 SQ3R

1 **S**urvey the text to ascertain the gist or general idea.
2 **Q**uestion – while surveying the text, think about questions that you would like the text to answer if you decide it is relevant to read in more detail.
3 **R**ead the text carefully if you think it is pertinent for your research.
4 **R**ecall the main points after you have read the text.
5 **R**eview the text to confirm that you have recalled all the main points that are significant for you and your work.

It is helpful, in addition to the SQ3R framework, to consider in more detail the techniques you might use to work through the above steps.

Survey: skim and scan A central purpose of surveying a text is to identify whether it is relevant for you to read in depth. To do this, skim (read quickly) some or all of the parts which signal the main points: the title, the blurb on the back of a book, the contents page, the index, the abstract of a journal article, the introduction and conclusion of a text, the first and last paragraphs of chapters, and the first and last sentences of paragraphs. After skimming, you should be in a good position to decide whether the source is suitable for a more comprehensive reading.

If you are looking for a specific piece of information in a text, you can scan to find what you require. This means reading quickly until you find the precise detail that you need. For example, it could entail looking for key words in the index of a book to find specific page numbers which cover the topic you are searching for, or it might mean casting your eye over the text itself to spot key words which indicate coverage of the information you want. When you find the important point you are looking for, you can read this part more slowly and carefully. An everyday example of scanning is looking for a phone number in telephone directory or checking a train time on the screen at the railway station.

Question If you decide that a text is relevant for you, then it will be necessary to read it more slowly and carefully in order to remember and understand the content. To prepare yourself to read the text interactively, think about what you already know about the topic; if appropriate, personalise the topic by relating it to your own experience, and predict what you think the text is going to tell you by formulating questions that you hope it will answer.

Read and make connections As you read, make connections with other texts you have read and your own knowledge as this will enable you to understand and remember the new information more effectively. If you are finding it difficult to understand a text, it may be useful to go back to reading less complex material such as introductory textbooks on a topic to build up your background knowledge. This helps you to develop a framework within which to fit more complex information that is new to you.

The note-taking techniques suggested in the section below are relevant at this stage and it is important to find an approach which suits you. You may be in a position to annotate a hard copy of the text with key words in the margin and highlighter pens. If this is the case you may or may not decide to take additional notes as well. However, library books have to be returned, in which case note taking is imperative to help you recall the important information. For these occasions it is helpful if you have a tried and tested system which works for you (see following sections on Techniques for note taking and Making connections between different texts).

To aid your understanding of a text, it can be helpful to map out its organisational structure. We tend to have expectations about how a text will be organised which can help us find the information we need quickly. For example, we usually expect an introduction at the beginning which outlines the content of the text and a conclusion at the end which summarises the main points. There are likely to be minor changes in topic with each new paragraph and more major changes between sections. Section headings indicate the content to follow. In a scientific text, one might expect the following sequence of information: introduction, problem, hypotheses, methods and experiments, results, discussion and conclusion. When taking notes, it can be useful to make a diagram of the structure of the text to illustrate visually how the information connects together.

If you are finding it difficult to digest the content of a text and realise you have to keep rereading pages to extract the meaning, you may find it helpful to break it down into more manageable chunks. The length of a 'manageable chunk' will vary according to the density and language difficulty of the material. It might be a paragraph, a section or a chapter.

Recall and review After each manageable chunk, recall and review your reading by writing a sentence summarising what you have just read. This is likely to ensure you understand and remember the content of the text. Effective summarisation is discussed in detail (see Techniques for writing a summary).

Critical reading

In addition to ascertaining the main points that an author is trying to convey, it is important to adopt a questioning and analytical approach towards the material. To read critically and analytically, try to answer the following questions in relation to all the texts you use for your research.

- What is the author's central argument or main point, i.e. what does the author want you, the reader, to accept?
- What conclusions does the author reach?
- What evidence does the author put forward in support of his or her arguments and conclusions?
- Do you think the evidence is strong enough to support the arguments and conclusions, i.e. is the evidence relevant and wide reaching enough?
- Does the author make any unstated assumptions about shared beliefs with the readers?
- Can these assumptions be challenged?
- What is the background context in which the text was written? Does the cultural and historical context have an effect on the author's assumptions, the content and the way it has been presented?

Increasing your reading speed

Because of the quantity of reading you will have to do for your research, it is important to read as quickly as is comfortable for you without jeopardising your comprehension of the material. A very important way to speed up your reading overall is to adopt the efficient strategies outlined above so that you are reading in the right way for your purposes at a particular time: i.e. you skim when deciding if a text is relevant for you and read more slowly and carefully, taking notes or annotating, when reading a text in detail. But having said this, if you want to increase your speed generally, the following tips may be helpful:

- Avoid saying the words aloud to yourself as you read.
- Do not run your finger under the lines as you read them; instead, run your finger down the left hand margin of the text to encourage quicker movement of your eyes down the page.
- Endeavour to focus on groups of words as you read each line and not on one word at a time because your natural eye movements involve a series of jumps across the page, pausing to take in each group of words.
- Try not to back track over the text more than necessary. However, a certain amount of regression is a normal part of the reading process as we often look back to check our understanding.
- Attempt to guess the meanings of words you are not sure about. You can look them up in the dictionary later if they are important for your comprehension of the text.
- Vary your speed according to the importance of the information, i.e. slow down for important explanations and speed up for supporting details and examples.
- To increase your reading speed overall, practise as often as possible under timed conditions and complete comprehension questions and/or write summaries to check that you are maintaining a thorough understanding of the content.

Reasons for note taking

When taking notes, you may find it helpful to keep the following reasons for doing so in mind:

- to identify and understand the main points of a text;
- to aid recall;
- to use in later research and writing;
- to aid concentration;
- to make connections between different sources;
- to rearrange information for writing;
- to avoid plagiarism.

Avoiding plagiarism

To expand briefly on the final point above, there are a number of different ways in which plagiarism can occur but the type being referred to here is the use of a cited author's exact words with no or little attempt at rephrasing. Unless these words are part of a direct quotation, this is plagiarism even if the source author is acknowledged in the correct way. Although it may be suitable, on occasions, to use direct quotations when the exact words of a source text are used, their excessive use suggests that you are hiding behind the ideas of the quoted authors and that you do not fully understand their work. Therefore it is essential that you are able rephrase and summarise the points you are taking from source material.

The reasons for and the conventions of referencing, and the various meanings of plagiarism, are discussed in more detail in Chapter 7. Plagiarism is a practice which must be avoided because, in whatever way it occurs, it is considered to be 'literary theft' and suggests a lack of respect for the work of others. When plagiarism occurs, it can result in work being failed or even expulsion from a course of study. It is important to acknowledge the work of others in a respectful way following established conventions.

The suggestions for effective note taking and summarising in the next section provide tips which will assist you in using your own words and hence avoiding plagiarism in your writing.

Techniques for note taking

Features of effective notes

Effective notes are ones that are easy for you to understand at a later time. They generally make use of: key words, e.g. nouns, verbs, adjectives to represent important points; abbreviations and symbols; a system which shows clearly the difference between main and subsidiary points (this will help you see how the author's ideas all fit together), and a note of all your references.

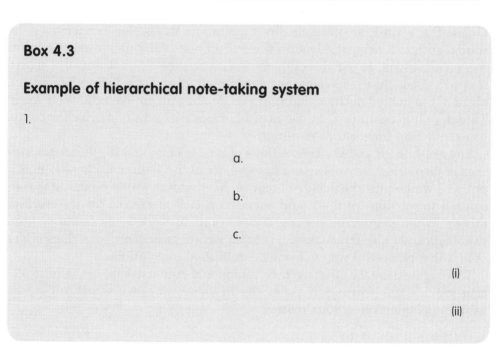

Box 4.2

Note taking – abbreviations and symbols

e.g.	for example
i.e.	in other words
cf.	compare with
n.b.	note well (important)
>	more than
<	less than
=	equal to
→	leads to

Box 4.3

Example of hierarchical note-taking system

1.

      a.

      b.

      c.

            (i)

            (ii)

Whichever system of note taking you use, it is vitally important that you record all the details of the reference that you are citing. Make a note of every detail that you will need for the bibliography so that you do not have to search for any of the information at a later stage. If you are including direct quotations, page numbers are essential. In Chapter 5, some of the choices available for keeping records and organising the information that you read are discussed. In addition, more details are provided on writing bibliographies.

Three main formats for note taking

Annotating a hard copy of the text If you have your own copy of a text, use a high-lighter pen to mark significant points. Write key words in the margins to signal important items. You can use different coloured high-lighter pens for different types of information: for example, you could use one colour for the main idea of a paragraph and another for key examples or supporting information. A third colour could be used for your own comments on the material in the text. Use Post-it stickers to mark important pages in a book.

Pattern notes These take the form of a spider diagram or a mind map, where you put the central idea in the middle of the page and branch out from this with the main themes and sub-themes of the text that you are reading (see Figure 4.1). Mind mapping software such as Mind Genius (http://www.mindgenius.com/) is available if you prefer to do this type of activity electronically. MindGenius has a facility whereby you can set up prompt questions, such as those suggested for critical reading, and address these as you create your mind map.

Linear notes Use headings and subheadings to distinguish between the main ideas and the subsidiary information in a text (see Example 4.1 below).

Your own comments

In whatever form you take your notes, it is important to include your own comments; however, it is also essential to distinguish clearly between the ideas from the text and your own observations. Use a different coloured pen, or font colour if using the computer, to write down your own comments and thoughts about what you are reading: your opinions and questions about the text; connections with your research or other texts you have read; ideas inspired by what you are reading.

It is beneficial to write both a summary of a text and then a short critical review (based on responses to the questions in the section on critical reading above). This will help you recall the content of the text, making it easier to locate the relevant pieces of information and references that you need when you begin to write your literature review.

Another electronic tool that can be helpful for recording information is a digital notebook such as *OneNote*. This is a free-form note-taking facility available as part of Microsoft Office (http://office.microsoft.com/en-us/onenote/). It is a flexible tool allowing you to store text, pictures, drawings, and audio and video recordings; these can be arranged as you wish on the page. There is great potential for using this tool to make notes on your reading, incorporating your own spoken reactions and drawings as well as more conventional pattern or linear notes. Another similar piece of software that my students have recommended is *Evernote* (http://www.evernote.com/). It was launched in 2008 and has a free version which can be downloaded onto your computer or smart phone.

Handwritten notes vs computer notes

There are some advantages to using a computer system for your notes, whether this is in a specifically tailored package such as EndNote or Reference Manager (see Chapter 5), with mind mapping software, or through the creation of your own system using digital notebooks (OneNote; Evernote), word processing or database files. First, on a computer package there are search facilities which enable you to look for key words within your notes and locate relevant information quickly. Second, you can copy and paste details such as the bibliographical information easily. Third, you can move information around quickly, re-categorising ideas and making new connections.

There are also some dangers, however. With the copy and paste function it is easy to miss the redrafting and rewording stages which are essential for developing your ideas and avoiding plagiarism. If you are using a program such as EndNote you do need to invest time into getting to know the package and if you want all your notes to be on the computer you will need a laptop or smart phone to have with you at all times to accommodate all the occasions on which you may wish to take notes. However, the advantages of storing information electronically are considerable so it is well worth giving some thought to the way you can use the computer and the relevant software to the best effect for your purposes.

But notwithstanding all the new technologies available, it is still invaluable to carry round a small notebook at all times to jot down the ideas that occur to you, for example, when suddenly waking at 3 a.m. or when waiting at a bus stop. These thoughts can then be incorporated into your more systematic note-taking records when appropriate.

Making connections between different texts: using key words

Matching key words that you have devised to identify main points in different texts can help you make links between topics mentioned in the various sources of information that you read. Often, you will notice contradictions or differences in the literature in relation to research findings or the way theories and terminology are interpreted and used. By writing key words in the margins of your source texts or as headings in your notes, you will be able to find your way quickly to the references or parts of a text where a particular topic is discussed. Observing these connections between different references and making them explicit in your writing is all part of being a critical researcher. In Chapter 6, I show how these connections become relevant when deciding on the structure of your literature review and selecting the different sources that you will use to support the various steps in the argument that you develop in your review.

It is therefore important to work out a system for cross-referencing between the key words identified in your notes on different texts so that you can effectively integrate ideas from different sources in your writing. Again you face the choice between a computer or paper-based system.

A system of note cards is recommended by some (Bell, 2010: 71; Blaxter et al., 2010: 121; Walliman, 2011: 66). If using cards, I would recommend one set of cards for bibliographical details of each reference (see Chapter 5) and another for notes of key points taken from each reference. For the latter set of cards, you can identify the text that the notes are from by writing the author's name and date of publication at the top of the card. As a means of facilitating the shift from reading to writing, if you record one piece of information on each note card, with a clear reference of where it has come from, you can file this information under key words to make connections between texts. When preparing to write, you can lay all your cards out on the floor and shift around the order of the information you want to include. This is a useful way of working out the structure and organisation of your literature review.

You may feel, however, that a system of note cards seems quite laborious and time consuming when computer packages are available with quick and efficient key word search facilities. Nevertheless, your available floor space is probably bigger than your computer screen and therefore physically spreading out and moving around your note cards may give you more flexibility when organising your ideas for your writing. It may be that you adopt a computer based note-taking system at first when you are reading widely and exploring ideas and then consider putting the most relevant points onto note cards when formulating your arguments for your written review (see Chapter 6).

A software package such as NVivo (http://www.qsrinternational.com/products_nvivo.aspx) which is principally known as a tool for the collation, coding and analysis of qualitative data can be invaluable for making connections between different source texts. It offers more sophisticated analysis techniques than those available on reference manager applications, such as EndNote. This application allows you to analyse the literature in a similar way to the analysis of qualitative data by adding codes to your notes. Within NVivo you can run 'queries' to search for themes across your sources, thus helping you make connections between key words across your references and note the similarities and differences between the ideas of authors being cited. You can either import bibliographical information and your notes about your literature from a reference manager tool such as EndNote (see Chapter 5) or you can take notes directly into NVivo for each source that you read.

Making connections between texts: a tabular comparison

A technique commonly recommended by supervisors to help you achieve an overview of the sources that you are reading is the creation of a table in which you record key information from a group of articles. Recording information in this way enables you to make quick comparisons between studies identifying similarities and differences. The table can provide a helpful stepping stone for the writing especially when reviewing a number of empirical research studies on a similar theme, e.g. investigations into the uses of students' first language in a second language learning class-room. Extracting key information in this way from a source encourages you to be concise and focus on the essential information for comparing and contrasting across references. Sample headings for a table are shown below.

TABLE 4.1   A tabular comparison of sources

Articles on the theme of:

Author/s (year)	Aims or research questions	Location of study	Sample size and identity	Data collection methods	Key findings

However, prior to a tabular comparison, it is strongly recommended that you take notes in a more detailed manner on each source text either on paper, or using a mind map, digital notebook, reference management software, or NVivo. This ensures you have recorded more detail if needed later on as you progress with your research.

Techniques for writing a summary

Reading is closely connected to the writing process. This connection starts when you annotate, take notes and write summaries of the texts that you read. The close relationship continues while you draft and redraft your dissertation or thesis.

A summary is a concise synopsis of a text which includes the main points of the original text as opposed to all the details. It is different from a paraphrase. When you write a paraphrase, all the information in a sentence or group of sentences from the original cited source is reworded. The aim is to rephrase everything and not to select the most important points. Although there may be occasions when you wish to paraphrase, it is more common to summarise when taking information from source texts as usually you will wish to be selective about the information you incorporate into your own writing.

There are different types of summary and the type you write will vary according to your purpose at a particular point.

A global summary

You may write a global summary when you summarise the entire contents of a text. Global summaries of the key texts you identify for your research are a good idea and provide a useful step between note taking and the selection and integration of source material into your writing. They help you identify what is important. By writing a summary, you become very familiar with the material so that you can recall significant points that you may want to come back to at a later stage in your research and when you are writing your literature review. It is an effective way of ensuring that you understand and remember what you read. It is also a helpful strategy for identifying where there are connections to be made between different source texts.

Abstracts of journal articles, dissertations and theses are global summaries which are created to introduce a reader to the content of the text which follows.

A selective summary

Selective summaries are written when you need to extract some relevant information from a small part of a text for a specific purpose. For example, you may be looking for a reference to support your argument that governments should change their policy on the use of renewable energy sources. In this case, you would not need to summarise entire source texts; rather you would use and acknowledge the parts that are significant for your argument.

Techniques

The following process may help you when writing a summary.

- Make a record of the main points of a text either by note taking or by highlighting and annotating.
- Produce the first draft of the summary by first of all acknowledging the source and then writing down the main points that the text is making.
- Redraft the summary to present the main points in the most logical order. This does not have to be in the same order as the original text. Check that you have not included more detail than is necessary for the purposes of your summary.
- Check back to the original text to ensure you have included all the main points that you need.
- Remember that in a summary you are reporting the author's main ideas. If you wish to make your own comments on the work, be careful to signal it clearly with a phrase such as, 'However, other researchers have found that … ' or 'But in my view … '.

Example 4.1 Linear notes, pattern notes and a global summary

The source text below is followed by some examples of note taking to illustrate both linear notes and pattern notes. Finally a global summary of the text is included.

The source extract

In contemporary U.S. society, many adolescents spend considerable amounts of time in online interactions (Subramanyam, Greenfield, Kraut, & Gross, 2002). The language used on the Internet demonstrates an evolution of discourse (Crystal, 2001), and adolescents are in the midst of that language evolution (Greenfield & Subramanyam, 2003). Sometimes referred to as netspeak, the language of the Internet entails both traditional linguistic forms and adapted ones that include slang and non-standard forms that are sometimes used in offline life. Netspeak is an emergent discourse that is shaped entirely by the creativity of its community (Crystal, 2001). The introduction of acronyms (e.g., 'lol = laugh out loud,' 'brb = be right back'), plays on variations on words (e.g., 'cya = see you', 'latah = later'), graphical icons that represent emotions, called emoticons (e.g., :) or ;-{}) or graphical icons that represent a real person in a virtual context, called avatars, are all examples of language produced by online communicators. This language continues to evolve and remains an important area of study when considering the ways in which Internet users interact and express who they are.

Scholars have actively explored how identity and language are manifested in online interactions. Current research in computer-mediated communication (CMC) environments such as chat rooms, newsgroups, and multi-user domains (MUDs) has revealed interesting trends in the way individual identity is presented, language is used, and interactions have transpired (Calvert, 2002; Crystal, 2001; Greenfield & Subramanyam, 2003; Herring, 2000; Turkle, 1995). Yet, as new Internet applications are created and embraced, CMC studies must continue to strive toward the understanding of online identity, language, and interaction.

Such is the case for weblogs or 'blogs.' Blogs are personal journals or reversed-chronological commentaries written by individuals and made publicly accessible on the web, and they have distinctive technological features that set them apart from other forms of CMC (Herring et al., 2004a; Huffaker, 2004b). These features include: 1) ease-of-use, as users do not need to know HTML or other web programming languages to publish onto the Internet; 2) ways to archive information and knowledge; 3) opportunities for others to comment or provide feedback for each blog post; and 4) links to other 'bloggers' to form online communities.

These features are especially important for constructing online identity. First, the lack of technical expertise needed to create or maintain blogs makes the application more accessible regardless of gender and age. Next, the ability to archive blog posts creates a way to scaffold on previous impressions and expressions; thus, constructing identity can be a continual process for adolescents, and one to which they can refer. Finally, when blog software offers ways to provide feedback or link to other bloggers, this can foster a sense of peer group relationships, another important aspect for the developing adolescent. In short, weblogs represent a new medium for computer-mediated communication and may offer insight into the ways in which adolescents present themselves online, especially in terms of self-expression and peer group relationships, both of which impact the construction of identity.

Source: Huffaker and Calvert, 2005: 2–3

 Linear notes

This example illustrates the use of headings and different layers of subheadings with indentations to indicate the main and subsidiary points from the source text above (Huffaker and Calvert, 2005). Key words are used in the headings and subheadings to capture the essence of the source text.

(Continued)

(Continued)

Adolescent Internet interactions

1 Weblog = blog = personal journal on a publicly available web page

   a) Relatively new forum for internet communictn

   b) Popular amongst teenagers

     (i)   Easy to create as no knowl. of prog. lang. req.

     (ii) Poss. to store postings

     (iii) Can post comments on others' blogs

     (iv) Links betwn blogs

2 Studies of online communctn include analysis of:

   a) Language

   b) Identity

   c) Interactions

3 Features of Internet lang. or 'Netspeak' – evolving with use

   a) Use of acronyms

   b) Word plays

   c) Emoticons (graphical icons)

   d) Avatars (picture icons)

4 Blogs provide forum for study of adolescent identity formation through analysis of:

   a) Self-presentation

   b) Interaction with peers

Source: notes taken from Huffaker and Calvert, 2005

Pattern notes

Figure 4.1 gives a more visual representation of the major themes and sub themes of the source text (Huffaker and Calvert, 2005). The main topic of the text is in the centre, with branches connecting to the more detailed information from the text. Connections are also made between some of the subsidiary points to show additional connections made in the source text.

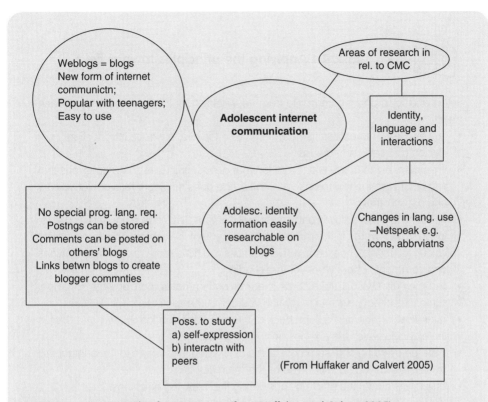

FIGURE 4.1   An example of pattern notes (from Huffaker and Calvert 2005)

A global summary

A global summary which summarises all the key information of a source text aids recall and ensures understanding. The example below gives an overview of the source extract provided above (Huffaker and Calvert, 2005).

eg → Huffaker and Calvert (2005) state that the study of Internet communication has been the focus of much recent research. They elaborate on how this research has included an examination of the construction of identity, the use of language, and the type of interactions that occur online. The focus of some studies has been on the development of Netspeak which is an evolving Internet language that includes icons and abbreviations. A relatively new site for data collection in this area has come about with the development of blogs or weblogs, an innovative type of Internet communication which is particularly popular among teenagers. Blogs are easy to use and require no specialist knowledge of a programming language. They are therefore likely to offer a suitable site for the analysis of adolescent identity formation as the facility for blog postings on both one's own and others' blogs gives opportunities for self presentation and interaction with peers.

(Huffaker and Calvert, 2005)

Task 4.1 Applying the principles to your field

Select and read a research article from your field. Adopt the approach suggested below.

- Survey the text to assess its relevance. Skim the title, abstract, introduction, conclusion and section headings.
- If you decide the article is relevant for your needs, articulate some questions that you would like the text to answer. If the article does not seem relevant for you, try one or two others.
- Read the text more slowly and carefully. If it is your own copy, highlight key points, jot down key words in the margin to remind you of the content and, in a different colour, jot down connections with other texts you have read, or your own opinions and comments about what you are reading.
- You may also wish to take some linear or pattern notes, and/or write summary sentences of each section to remind yourself of the content.
- After finishing the article, look back at the questions you formulated and assess the extent to which the text has answered these.
- Write an overall global summary of the article and then return to the original text to ensure that you have covered all the main points.
- Critically evaluate the article by answering the following questions:
  a What is the author's main argument? What conclusions are drawn?
  b What evidence does the author put forward to support the argument and conclusion?
  c What is your view of this evidence? Can you spot any weaknesses in the methodology, the findings and the way that the conclusions are drawn?
  d Has the author made any implicit assumptions about shared beliefs which you, the reader, you might question?

Summary

To summarise, this chapter has considered:

- why we read;
- how we can read efficiently according to our purpose at a particular time;
- how to read interactively and critically;
- ways of increasing reading speed;
- techniques for note taking and summarising;
- the use of key words to make connections between different sources of information;
- tabular comparisons of source texts.

5

Reference management: keeping records and organising information

Chapter summary

This chapter discusses the importance of and techniques for:

- logging literature searches;
- recording bibliographical details of references;
- becoming familiar with the features of bibliographies;
- developing a filing system for organising notes and hard copies of key source texts;
- avoiding copyright infringement.

In addition, the value and functionality of computer software packages which have specific referencing facilities, such as EndNote, ProCite, RefWorks and Reference Manager, are considered.

Managing the process

In order to manage the literature effectively it is essential to keep records. There are three types of record keeping system which are particularly helpful and you are advised to develop:

- a record of all the key word searches that you do;
- a record of all the bibliographical details you will need for your list of references at the end of your dissertation or thesis;
- a personal library: a filing system of hard copies and/or notes of key texts.

A record of key word searches

As recommended in Chapter 3, it is well worth keeping a log of all the key word searches that you undertake. It is easy to get carried away when doing searches on different databases and catalogues, trying out many variations and different combinations of your choice of key words without pausing to make notes on what you are doing. Without any record of what you have tried out, at a later stage, it will be very difficult to remember exactly where and how you did these searches. It is quite possible that you will duplicate your work and do the same searches again. Thus, a log of all the key word combinations you have tried will enable you to work more efficiently and avoid needless repetition.

Of course, you may intend to repeat your searches if you are looking to see whether there have been any new publications in a field and in this situation as well it is helpful to have a record of the searches conducted previously. By looking back at your records of earlier searches you will be able to revisit databases and catalogues which you have identified as useful in the past and remind yourself of the key word combinations that were successful on prior occasions.

In order for your records to be comprehensive, they should include notes of:

- the key words, phrases and Boolean search terms you used;
- the date that you carried out the search;
- the search engines, databases and catalogues in which you conducted each search;
- the results you obtained from each search.

These records can be kept manually in a notebook, in a Word file or on an electronic database such as Excel (see Table 3.1 for a checklist). You can adopt the format which suits your style of working and preference (or not) for technology. Although it may sometimes seem laborious to keep a log such as this up to date, it can be a real time saver in the long run. It is also interesting to look back over your records at a later date and see how the direction and focus of your search strategy gradually evolved as your research project developed. Electronic applications and databases may have facilities for keeping a record of your key word searches so it is a good idea to use 'help' menus rigorously and explore all tabs to see what is possible.

Additionally, on your notes or hard copies of articles you may find it helpful and interesting to make a note of the path that led you to the reference, e.g. it was found from a bibliography in a particular book, from browsing the new issues of journals in the library, or from a key word search for, say, obesity AND teenagers on the Medline database.

A record of bibliographical details

A bibliography is the list at the end of your dissertation or thesis of books, journal articles, electronic references, and other source texts, which you have referred to in your work. The list may have a variety of different titles, for example bibliography; references; or work cited. Technically, a 'bibliography' can refer to all the source texts that you have referred to while doing your research whereas a list entitled 'references' includes only the references which are actually cited within the main body of the text in the dissertation or thesis. Generally speaking, at postgraduate level, you are expected to show how you have drawn on a particular source text, so in your list (whether entitled bibliography or references) it is common to include only those references which you refer to within the main body of the text. If you have any queries, consult your supervisor to check whether there are particular conventions that you should conform to with regard to the title and the sources which should be included in the list of references at the end of your dissertation or thesis.

As every researcher and librarian will remind you, it is vital to keep a record of all the bibliographical details of every source text that you think you will include in your bibliography. Hours can be wasted searching for an elusive journal name, article title or page number that is needed before the final draft of the work is complete. When there is a submission deadline to meet, it can be especially frustrating to be delayed by missing details for the bibliography.

It is important to familiarise yourself with the referencing conventions of your field so that you can keep a record of all the necessary details from the day you begin reading for your research. Your university web pages will provide details of the referencing expectations of your university and access to other web pages offering further advice. You should also consult any specific guidelines provided by your department as your discipline may have a preferred style and particular recommendations for types of sources that may be specific to your field, e.g. court cases in law or musical manuscripts in music.

Some general conventions which describe the information required in bibliographies for the most common types of information sources are included below.

81

A book Surname of author, initials of author, year of publication, *title in italics*, place of publication and publisher.

Example: Weart, S.R. (2003) *The Discovery of Global Warming*. Cambridge, Mass.: Harvard University Press.

A chapter in an edited collection or reader Surname of author, initials of author, year of publication, title of chapter (in single quote marks), initials of editor, surname of editor, (ed. or eds), *title of book in italics*, place of publication and publisher.

Example: Scott, M. (1999) 'Agency and subjectivity in student writing', in C. Jones, J. Turner and B. Street (eds) *Students Writing in the University: Cultural and Epistemological Issues*. Amsterdam/Philadelphia: John Benjamins Publishing Company.

A journal article Surname of author, initials of author, year of publication, title of article (in single quote marks), *name of journal in italics,* volume/ issue: page numbers.

Example: Shield, F., Enderby, P. and Nancarrow, S. (2006) 'Stakeholder views of the training needs of an interprofessional practitioner who works with older people', *Nurse Education Today,* 26/5: 367–76.

A thesis, dissertation, or project Surname of author, initials of author, year of submission, title of thesis (within single quote marks), level of degree, place of submission.

Example: O'Hanlon, B. (2005) 'Mobile technology for housing association repair departments'. UG final year project, University of Leeds.

Electronic references There are many different types of electronic reference so look for more detailed guidelines on your library web page. Two general principles to keep in mind are: first, you should include enough information for a reader to be able to track down the citation and, second, in order that you cover yourself in case the electronic reference is no longer available, you should include the date that you accessed the information. If possible, all the following information should be included: surname of author, initials of author, year of publication, title of text, URL address, and date accessed.

Example: The Higher Education Academy (2006) Curriculum Design http://www.heacademy.ac.uk/795.htm (accessed: July 22 2006).

As noted in Chapter 3, you must be careful to evaluate the credibility of any electronic reference that you cite. If you cannot identify the individual or organisation who wrote the text, it is probably not a reliable source to be using in an academic context.

The details of punctuation used in bibliography entries vary but the golden rule is to be consistent. One way to decide on the precise format to follow is to consult an important journal in your field and follow their style. All journals have guidelines for authors which describe their exact requirements for the layout of bibliographies. I would recommend that you always have a copy of the guidelines you are going to follow close to hand until you are familiar with the exact information you need to record, and the punctuation and layout that you are going to adopt.

To record these bibliographical details as you refer to sources of information, you could create a file in Word, use a referencing software package such as EndNote or Reference Manager, or create manual records using note cards (see Chapter 4). EndNote is described in more detail below, showing how it can be helpful when recording the details of different types of references.

If you are likely to include direct quotations in your dissertation or thesis, it is essential that you also record the page numbers in the book or article the quote has been taken from. Ensure you have the exact wording of the quote if you do not have a hard copy of the source text to refer to. The page numbers are not required in the bibliography but they must be included in the text when the quote is used. Conventions for in-text citations are discussed in detail in Chapter 7.

Where you refer to two different publications by the same author/s which were published in the same year, the one mentioned first in the main text should include a lower case 'a' after the year, e.g. (Hyland 2010a) and the second one a 'b', e.g. (Hyland 2010b). The entries in the bibliography should correspond to the in-text references and include 2010a and 2010b after the author's name for each entry, as illustrated below.

Hyland, K. (2010a) 'Constructing proximity: relating to readers in popular and professional science', *Journal of English for Academic Purposes,* 9/2: 116–27.

Hyland, K. (2010b) 'Community and individuality: performing identity in Applied Linguistics', *Written Communication,* 27/2: 159–88.

Another query frequently raised by students is that of secondary references, i.e. when you cite an author whose work you have not yet seen but who was cited in a source that you *have* read. In this scenario, the in-text reference must make it explicit that the citation is a secondary reference, e.g. (Bhatia 1993, cited in Hyland 2010). The Hyland 2010 reference is included in the bibliography and the Bhatia 1993 secondary citation is not.

The order of the entries in a bibliography can vary. For example, some science and engineering fields may require a numerically ordered bibliography, in which the number for each reference indicates the order in which the references are first cited in the text. However, the majority of disciplines use the Harvard system and will require alphabetical bibliographies where the references are sequenced alphabetically according to the first letter of the author's surname. As described below, EndNote has a facility for creating bibliographies in the style required.

A personal library

The third type of record keeping system which is crucial for your research is a classification scheme for coding and filing hard copies of the texts you collect and identify as being relevant to your research. It is useful to download or photocopy important articles and key chapters from books so that you can refer back to the originals. If this is not possible, make sure you take comprehensive notes and file the notes from these sources. Without a filing system of some kind it will become very difficult to keep track of your references, and as the pile of photocopied articles grows higher and higher on your desk, it will become increasingly difficult to find a text when you want to refer to it again.

To create a coding system, break your topic of research down into subsections and file the literature accordingly in box files or folders. On the cover of the folder, write a name for the category and record quick references to the articles/chapters included inside, either by using author names and/or the article/chapter titles. You can number your folders and use a system of cross-referencing to another folder if a particular reference is relevant in two categories. Although it can become costly, some researchers even like to photocopy multiple copies of key articles so that they can store them in their files for more than one category (but see section on copyright below).

If you have both your own notes and hard copies of articles, you may prefer to develop a separate filing system for each. However, I have found that it is more straightforward to work with a single filing system for both my notes and the original texts so if I take linear or pattern notes of a text and/or write a summary of it, I staple these to my hard copy of an article and file them together. Alternatively, if using EndNote or another electronic application, you can make your notes and write your summary on the computer as part of your electronic entry for each reference. However, you do need to be careful to distinguish between your own notes and summaries and those that you download electronically with the reference. I would strongly recommend using a different coloured font for your own notes if made electronically. You can access your notes quickly by conducting key word searches or opening up the particular reference to which the notes apply. This particular function of EndNote is discussed in a later section.

Copyright legislation

When using source material for your research, it is important to be aware of and avoid contravention of copyright legislation. This is relevant in relation to Internet material, articles and chapters in books that you may wish to download or photocopy for reference whilst conducting your research. It could also be important if you wish to make extensive use of copied maps, illustrations, tables or similar items, especially if they are from a single source, in your dissertation or thesis.

The Copyright, Designs and Patents Act 1988 provides the basis of copyright legislation in the UK although a number of European copyright directives have also now been incorporated within it. This legislation protects intellectual property when it appears in a physical format, e.g. publications, literary works, computer programs, databases, web pages, art work, sculptures, musical scripts, song lyrics, audio and video recordings, films and broadcasts. The law gives the creator of the work or the copyright owner the right to allow or prevent the copying, reproduction (or performance) of the work and the right to be acknowledged as the author or designer. This right to protection is automatic once the work is committed to paper or another physical form; i.e. registration of the work is not required in the same way as it would be for a patent for an original invention or a trademark.

However, there is an exception to this protection which comes within the scope of 'fair dealing'; it is permissible to make single copies of short extracts (one chapter in a book or one article in a journal issue) of publications as part of research for non-commercial purposes, for educational reasons and for personal use as long as the work and its creator are acknowledged. If accessing an ebook, you will be able to download a prescribed number of pages. Thus, when creating your library of resources for your own research, copyright legislation allows you to copy single copies of extracts of publications within certain limits. In addition, any published work (apart from photographs) may be reproduced for the purposes of review, critique and the reporting of current events. The material must also be acknowledged although this is not a requirement for films, recordings and broadcasts.

There are exceptions to the above rules for those who are visually impaired or have poor hearing. Adaptations can be made to scripts or recordings to enable access for all users of the material.

For more extensive copying of source material, permission must be sought from the copyright owner. For example, in your dissertation or thesis, you might want to reproduce a number of maps or diagrams from a specific source. The copyright owner will be the person who created the work or the publisher of a book or journal. In some circumstances, it may be the creator's employer, for example, if the work has been created as part of the contract of employment. A small fee may need to be paid to the copyright owner for the use of the material and acknowledgement of the work and its creator must be included in the reproduction.

Universities and other educational institutions may purchase licences which can be obtained from an organisation such as the Copyright Licensing Agency to allow multiple copying from specified sources over a period of time. Nevertheless, there are still strict guidelines as to the amount of material and number of copies that can be made. Permission usually includes up to 5 percent of a work, one article per journal, one chapter per book, one paper from conference proceedings, and one case from a publication of judicial proceedings. The numbers copied should not exceed the number of students on a course and one tutor. Universities may also hold a license to digitise copies of book chapters and journal articles for use with students and licences for recordings and newspaper articles or extracts. Librarians will be able to advise you as to what is permissible under the licences that a particular university holds.

The following web sites provide further information about copyright legislation and should be consulted if you have any concerns about copyright in relation to your own research:

The Copyright Licensing Agency   http://www.cla.co.uk/
Intellectual Property Office   http://www.ipo.gov.uk/

Bibliographical software packages

To assist you in the management of your references, it is a good idea to consider the computer software packages available There is a basic reference management tool available on Microsoft Word (located under the 'References' tab) which may well provide the functionality that you need, for example, if conducting a small-scale research project. This offers the facility to store bibliographical details of the references that you are using, insert citations as you write, and automatically create a bibliography according to your preferred style. However, there are more sophisticated applications available which should also be considered.

I have already referred to EndNote a number of times, indicating some of its functions and when it could be a helpful tool. If you do decide to use reference management software, I would strongly advise that you spend some time early on in the research process exploring its potential and becoming familiar with how to use it. For example, if you are going to store details of all your references in EndNote, it is important to start doing this from the beginning of your research when you first start identifying source texts. If you wait until you are two years into your research, it is a much more arduous procedure to transfer all your records into EndNote libraries.

Bibliographical software packages enable you to:

- fill in a record for each reference using an appropriate and flexible template for each reference type;
- store and organise your references into electronic libraries;
- use the drag and drop function to move references around between libraries;
- input your own notes and summaries for each of your references;
- conduct key word searches for common themes among the references in each of your libraries; searches can be field specific, e.g. according to author, year or key word/s.

- download references and their bibliographical details from electronic catalogues, data-bases and journals;
- include electronic links to the full text of articles in each reference record;
- conduct searches in remote catalogues and databases;
- include citations from your 'libraries' as you write in Word;
- create bibliographies in your preferred style;
- share your 'libraries' with other researchers.

There are a number of different packages available. The introductory web pages to four important ones are:

- EndNote: http://www.endnote.com/
- Reference Manager: http://www.refman.com/
- ProCite: http://www.procite.com/
- RefWorks http://www.refworks.com/

Your university is likely to support one of the above, thereby enabling you to access the software either free of charge or at a small cost. Look on your library web page or consult staff in the library or computer centre to find out which one is available and how you are able to access it. Alternatively, you can go to one of the above web sites for a demonstration of each package and details of how to purchase it. New versions of each of these bibliographical software packages with additional features are created and launched regularly; for example, mobile applications are now available whereby you can access your bibliographical files when you are on the move through your phone as long as you have Internet access.

As mentioned in the previous chapter, reference manager software can be used in conjunction with the powerful information handling and data analysis tool, NVivo. Bibliographical data can be exported from the reference manager application to NVivo to use the analysis tools for developing and organising your literature review. It can also be helpful to add the bibliographical data to a research project in progress on NVivo. When writing up your project, the references can be imported back into the reference manager application so that you can use the 'write and cite' and bibliography formatting tools which are not available in NVivo.

Using EndNote: the main functions

As an example of a reference manager application, the basic functions and advantages of Endnote are described here. If you do purchase or obtain access to this package, detailed guidelines are provided for its use. But be prepared; the user guide consists of over 600 pages of advice so you will probably wish to refer to it selectively. I outline the main functions of the package and give some tips about how you can start using it. However, you will need to consult the EndNote user guide or instructions provided by your own university for more detailed help. I would suggest that you select the functions that are useful for your purposes rather than use every facility that the package offers. More recent versions of the package may vary and offer additional features but the basic functionality remains the same. For whichever bibliographical software you decide to use, you will find a 'help' tab within it which will assist you to make a start and offer solutions to questions that arise as you go along.

Reference libraries for storing details of your references Within EndNote you can create database files called 'Reference libraries' in which you can store individual references. To create a new library, select 'Create a new EndNote Library' from the opening window of the Endnote program (see Screenshot 5.1). By creating a selection of libraries with different names you can categorise your reading into topic areas. If this screen does not appear when you open EndNote, go to the *File* menu and select *New* or *Open* to create a new library or open an existing library.

SCREENSHOT 5.1   © 2012 Thomson Reuters

Within the reference libraries you can store all the bibliographical information you need for each reference that you wish to use for your research. For each different reference type (for example, a journal article, a book, government document), EndNote provides a set of fields which are appropriate for this specific reference type. For example, for a journal article, you fill in the following fields: Author/s, Year of publication, Title of article, Name of the journal, Volume, Issue and Page numbers. There are also a number of other fields such as those which enable you to include the abstract of an article, incorporate an electronic link to the article itself, or add your own notes (see Screenshot 5.2).

SCREENSHOT 5.2 © 2012 Thomson Reuters

EndNote provides you with the facility to edit the fields available for each reference type:

- Choose 'Preferences' from the 'Edit' menu.
- From the list which appears on the left of the EndNote preferences box, select 'Reference Types'.
- From the drop-down list on the right of the box, choose the Reference Type that you wish to change, e.g. 'Newspaper article'.
- Click on 'Modify Reference Type'.
- In the column on the right in the new box which appears (see Screenshot 5.3), you can delete, rename or add fields.
- You have the option of applying the field change to all reference types which you can do by clicking on the 'Apply to All Ref Types' button.
- Click 'OK' to save your changes.

Key word searches It is possible to locate references stored in Endnote quickly and efficiently through key word searches.

- Open a reference library.
- If the search boxes are not visible in the lower half of the screen, click on 'show Tab Pane' in the bottom right hand corner.
- Select a key word or phrase and specify the fields that you want to search, e.g. the 'Title' field.
- It is possible to use the Boolean search terms, And, Or and Not to make your search either more specific or more wide reaching.

SCREENSHOT 5.3   © 2012 Thomson Reuters

For example, the search shown in Screenshot 5.4 is for any reference which includes within any of its fields, either of the words 'assessment' or 'testing' in conjunction with the term 'higher education'.

Importing references – manual data entry You can import references into these libraries either manually or by importing them from other electronic bibliographical databases. To enter a new reference manually into a reference library:

- Select 'New reference' from the 'References' menu, or click on the new reference icon on the tool bar.
- Select a 'Reference type', such as, a journal article or a book, from the drop-down menu.
- EndNote offers you fields to fill in which are appropriate for that reference type, as shown in Screenshot 5.2.

You can add your own notes and key words to the bibliographical entries to identify a source text. I would strongly recommend using a different coloured font for your own additions, so that at a later date you can clearly distinguish between your comments and those written by the author of the source text. This confusion is most likely to arise when you import electronic references from electronic journals or databases as the author's abstract and key words are usually automatically inserted into the appropriate fields.

Reference entries can be edited at any time by clicking on the reference in the reference library and moving your cursor to the field you wish to change.

Downloading references from remote databases When accessing electronic databases, catalogues or journals directly through your university

SCREENSHOT 5.4 © 2012 Thomson Reuters

library connections, you can often import the bibliographical details of your selected references directly into your EndNote libraries using EndNote's import filters. Not all databases will offer you this option, but the possibility of downloading information in this way is becoming more widespread all the time. The filters play an important role as, by selecting the right filter for the database or catalogue that you are accessing, you save the data in a way that is compatible with the EndNote fields for each reference type. The difficulty is that every remote database appears to have its own system for downloading references to packages such as EndNote, some of which are more straightforward than others. If you meet any problems, consult help menus and librarians for assistance.

Example 5.1 Downloading an electronic journal article details into your EndNote library

eg → To illustrate the procedure, this example lays out the steps necessary for downloading a reference to EndNote from an electronic journal. This type of process is becoming more and more common as information management becomes

(Continued)

(Continued)

increasingly computer based. Where available, you can download all the bibliographical details that you need, the abstract and an electronic link to the article itself. The procedure generally involves marking the relevant article with a tick in the box beside its title in the contents page of the journal and then selecting the 'Export' button (see Screenshot 5.5).

SCREENSHOT 5.5   http://www.sciencedirect.com

You usually then have the option of selecting EndNote which, if loaded onto your computer, will automatically open. You select the reference library into which you want the details of the article to go and the reference downloads automatically (see Screenshot 5.6).

SCREENSHOT 5.6   http://www.sciencedirect.com

Screenshot 5.7 shows an example of the reference as it appears in the EndNote reference library.

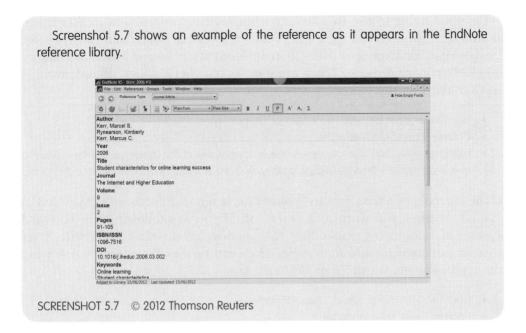

SCREENSHOT 5.7   © 2012 Thomson Reuters

Conducting searches in remote catalogues and databases You can also connect to a large number of online catalogues and conduct key word searches from within EndNote and download references into your EndNote libraries. Once connected to a specific online catalogue, such as the British Library, you can carry out a key word search in the same way as you would within EndNote. From the references found in the catalogue, you can download the bibliographical details into your own Endnote libraries. However, you cannot specify the articles that you want to download and you still have to access the source text itself either through an interlibrary loan service or electronically if the article or book is available in this form.

There are some other drawbacks to be aware of when conducting searches of remote databases through EndNote. You do not have access to some of the facilities that would be available if you accessed the database directly. For example, when searching through EndNote you cannot access the advanced search features of the remote database or its online help menu and you do not see links to the full text of articles. Therefore, you are likely to find it preferable to access the electronic database, catalogue or journal directly and then import the references to EndNote.

Cite from EndNote while you write and create your own bibliography You can cite from your EndNote libraries while you write a document in Word. You may need to configure Word to work with EndNote, so consult the computer centre in your university on how to do this. If EndNote is loaded onto your computer and is already configured, 'EndNote' will appear on the toolbar when you are working in Word.

Before starting to use this facility while writing a document in Word, you should select and amend the bibliographical styles to that which you are most likely to use. EndNote has over 1,000 different styles stored which are mainly labelled by journal name. There are also some generic styles offered, such as 'author–date' or 'numbered'.

- In EndNote, from the 'Edit' menu, select 'Output' styles'.
- Choose 'Open Style Manager'.
- From the styles and journal names which appear, select the styles you are most likely to use and these will then be available when you are working both in EndNote and in Word.

If the journal style that you are looking for is not there, choose a style that is similar to what you want and *amend* it. If you are following the Harvard system of referencing, amending the generic *author–date* style with your specific punctuation and font preferences can be an effective way of getting the style that you want. To modify a style:

- From the 'Edit' menu, select 'Output Styles'.
- Choose 'Open Style Manager'.
- Click on the Style info/preview button to see examples of each style in the lower window.
- Change the setting from 'Style info' to 'Style preview'.
- Scroll through the styles and select the one you wish to edit, for example 'author–date', by clicking to place a tick in the box beside it and highlighting the full line.
- Click the 'Edit' button.
- When the 'Style Window' opens, from the 'File' menu, select 'Save as'.
- Choose a name for the new style. This will mean that the original style will remain unchanged for further use if necessary.
- In the left-hand column in the 'Style Window', select the aspect of the citation or the bibliography that you wish to change.
- For example, if you wish to change the way titles of books are written in bibliographies from being underlined to italics, click on 'template' under 'Bibliography'.
- In the window that appears, make the necessary changes.
- Click 'Save' from the 'File' menu and the amended style is available for use.

This procedure can be fiddly and it can take some time to get the citations and bibliography appearing exactly as you want but, once achieved, it can save you a lot of time in the long run.

Before you start writing in Word, it is a good idea to open EndNote and select the library you are going to be referencing from. To select the style that you want to use:

- From the toolbar in Word, select EndNote.
- Choose the style of referencing from the drop down menu that appears.

- Click on the Bibliography menu in the 'Format Bibliography' dialogue box, next to 'Format document', select the Word document you wish to format.
- Next to 'With output style' select the bibliographical style you want. The most common would be 'author–date'. If you have amended this style and given it a new name, select this one and click OK.

As you create a document, when you need to insert a citation:

1 From the 'Tools' menu in Word, select EndNote.
2 Choose 'Find Citation'.
3 In the 'Find' box you can either type a key word, an author surname or a year.
4 Click on 'Search'.
5 A list of items from the reference library which matches the search terms will appear.
6 Scroll down and select the one you need.
7 Click 'Insert'.
8 The reference will be inserted within your text.
9 As you write, EndNote automatically creates a bibliography for you at the end of the document in the style you have specified.

Creating an independent bibliography You can also create an independent bibliography which is not associated with a specific paper. This is likely to be the case when you wish to create the bibliography for your dissertation or thesis. In fact, you may well find this a more useful and straightforward way to create the bibliography that you need than the 'cite while you write' process outlined above. There are several different ways to create an independent bibliography, all of which are described in the EndNote user guide. One technique is outlined below to give an indication of the facility.

- Select the bibliographical style that you want by choosing 'Output Styles' from the 'Edit' menu.
- Select 'Open Style Manager'.
- Scroll down and select the style that you want.
- To do this, highlight the style, ensure the box is ticked beside it, and close the 'Style Manager' window by clicking on the cross in the right-hand corner.
- As above, if you have amended a style for your own personal use, select this one.
- Open the library from which you wish to create your bibliography. You may find it helpful to create a specific reference library which will form the basis of the bibliography for your dissertation or thesis.
- Select all the references that you wish to export to your bibliography by holding down the 'Shift' key.
- From the 'File' menu in EndNote, select 'Export'.

- From the 'Save File as Type' list, choose RTF (Rich Text Format) if you wish to create an editable Word document.
- Enter a file name and select the folder in which you wish to save your references.
- Click 'Save'.

Task 5.1 Record keeping for your own research

In the light of the issues raised in this chapter, consider your own record keeping systems for the literature you will be consulting throughout your research. Use the following checklist to reflect on how you are currently working and consider how you could develop your practice.

Literature record checklist

- ☐ I am keeping a record of all my key word searches.
- ☐ I have identified useful catalogues, databases, journals and authors that I will continue to refer to during my research.
- ☐ I have implemented a system for recording the bibliographical details of all the references I consult.
- ☐ I am aware of and have an example of the bibliographical conventions of my field, both for in-text citations and the bibliography.
- ☐ I am beginning to categorise my reading into topic areas.
- ☐ I have developed a filing system for storing my notes and hard copies of source texts.
- ☐ I have explored the potential of an electronic referencing package supported by my university (e.g. RefWorks, Reference Manager, ProCite, or EndNote).

I am using the above reference management software to do the following:

- ☐ Store references in reference libraries
- ☐ Keep my own notes on references
- ☐ Download electronic references
- ☐ Create my bibliography
- ☐ Other _____

Summary

To summarise, this chapter has looked at ways of managing the references that you use for your research. In particular, we have emphasised the importance of keeping records and developing a filing system for:

- key word searches;
- bibliographical details of all your references;
- your notes and hard copies of the source texts that you use.

An overview was also given of the significance of copyright law and the potential uses of referencing software packages, including guidance on how to implement the following functions in EndNote:

- the creation of electronic reference libraries;
- the manual input of bibliographical details and notes for references into EndNote libraries;
- key word searches within EndNote libraries;
- the download of references from electronic databases, catalogues and journals;
- searches in remote databases and download references;
- the citation of references from EndNote libraries while writing a document in Word;
- the modification of a citation and bibliographical style to suit personal requirements;
- the creation of an independent bibliography from an EndNote reference library.

Acknowledgement

EndNote X5 © 2012 Thomson Reuters.

6

Structuring the literature review

Chapter summary

This chapter considers:

- the cyclical nature of all the activities involved in the creation of a literature review;
- the close relationship between the processes of reading and writing;
- ways of structuring the review;
- the complementary relationship between the introduction and the literature review;
- some examples from theses and dissertations which illustrate how different researchers organise their use of the literature.

The processes involved in the creation of a literature review

Searching for the literature, reading the source material and writing the review are all interconnected and cyclical processes. There is no clear cut-off point when one activity ends and another begins. Indeed, although there may be an intensive focus on the literature review in the earlier weeks and months of a research project, the processes connected with the review continue to be interwoven throughout the research project. In particular, Wellington et al. (2005) emphasise the significance of continually revisiting the research questions or research focus to help you determine and adapt more precisely what and how much you read in relation to your research topic. Figure 6.1 illustrates the continuous, cyclical and interconnected processes which all contribute to the literature review. The literature searching, reading and writing feed into each other constantly; and all the other activities, such as formulating research questions and justifying the research problem, influence and are influenced by the literature searching and reading, providing inspiration for the writing. Your writing in turn helps you discover and clarify your ideas and can result in the refinement of the focus of your research and the content of your review.

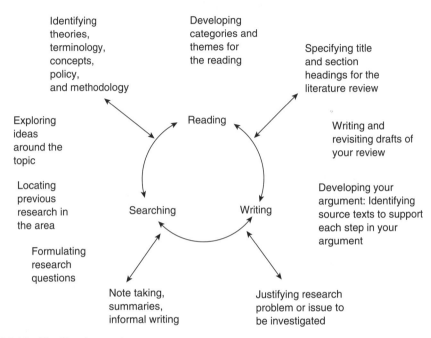

FIGURE 6.1   The literature review process

Beginning to write

It is a good idea to begin writing about the literature as early as possible and it definitely is not necessary to wait until you have a finalised plan or outline. Indeed, starting to write about the literature before the overall organisational structure of your review is clear in your mind is a means of helping you to understand the literature, and discover and clarify how you want to use it (see the sections on note taking and summarising in Chapter 4). In this vein, Murray (2011: 110) suggests various techniques to guide informal writing about the literature before moving on to more formal structured writing. She recommends regular writing to prompt questions, such as: 'What do I know about my research topic?'; 'What I am looking for in the literature is … '; 'What are the schools of thought in the literature?'; 'The "great debates" in my area are … '.

This type of regular writing is a means of establishing what you already know, identifying what further reading you need to do, clarifying how your research links with that of others, and developing your own understanding and interpretation of the literature. Some of your informal writing may form the basis of drafts for your actual literature review which will appear in your dissertation or thesis.

The structure of the literature review

Gradually, as your reading, note taking, summarising and informal writing progresses, you should try to pull together the various threads and move towards an arrangement with headings and subheadings to provide a framework for your review. The categories that you develop to organise your reading material can often provide the basis for the outline of your written review. You will have your own preference for the stage at which you devise an outline for your literature review; some researchers like to do this very early on in the process whereas others prefer to spend longer exploring the literature in a more free-ranging way. But at whatever point you decide on an outline, it will almost certainly change and evolve through a series of drafts.

Because every piece of research is different, it is difficult to suggest a common organisational structure but some suggestions are given below to help you think about the possibilities. The important point to remember is that in your review you should present a logical argument that leads smoothly into your own research, justifying both the need for work and the methodology that is going to be used.

Even if the review is not presented in a single chapter and you integrate your citations fairly evenly throughout the thesis, it is still helpful to make it clear to your reader how and where you address the various issues which have come from your reading. If integrating the literature in this continuous way, an overview of your approach in the introduction of the dissertation or thesis as well as appropriate headings and subheadings in the different chapters throughout the text is recommended.

For the more conventional and still more common practice of writing your literature review in one or more distinct chapters, it is strongly recommended that you include the following:

- an introduction which explains how your review is organised;
- headings and subheadings that provide a map to show the various strands of your argument;
- a summary where the key arguments are reiterated in a concise way.

If the review is long, as is likely for a PhD thesis, summaries interspersed throughout the chapter are helpful; these explain what you have argued so far and how this connects with what follows. An example of a 'transition statement' between sections is given in Example 6.1. The researcher refers to what she has discussed and makes a link with the relevant literature that she is going to address next. The italics indicate the signalling language which informs the reader about how the text is organised.

Example 6.1 The transition between sections

eg → *Having defined* comfortable intelligibility as a target in pronunciation for learners, *the next question to be addressed is* how we can help learners to achieve this. The teaching profession believes that instruction does help; however an intuitive belief is not reason enough to plan a course of instruction. *The next section will look briefly at* research on the effects of second language instruction in general *and then turn to* the area of pronunciation instruction in particular.

Source: Moore, 2001: 5

Although it is impossible to prescribe a uniform structure for a literature review, there are some organisational principles which are followed by many research writers. You may draw on a combination of the different approaches mentioned below depending on which is most suitable for each particular part of your review.

Weissberg and Buker (1990: 45–6) propose three ways for ordering citations:

1 Distant to close
   Most distantly related to your work→Most closely related to your work
2 Chronological
   Earliest related work→Most recent related work
3 Comparison and contrast of different approaches or particular features or characteristics of relevant theories and research
   One approach→An alternative approach→Another approach

In relation to the first of these approaches, Rudestam and Newton (2007) talk about long shots, medium shots and close-ups to describe the different degrees of depth that you may go into when referring to source texts according to their closeness and relevance to your research. Long shots describe the references that provide the background context to the research. These references tend to be quite general, acknowledging that research has been done on the topic without going into detail. Medium shots are the references which have more bearing on the current research and although not critiqued in detail, enough information is given to show how they impact on the proposed

101

research. The close-ups are the references that are particularly pertinent for the proposed research and include a critical examination of the work cited. For example, it might be that a limitation in a study cited provides the basis for your research question in which case you would have to do a detailed critique of the study to show how your work connects to it.

I often advise research students who are uncertain about the best way to structure their literature review to think of it as having two distinct but related parts: one which presents the current state of knowledge in the field where your research is situated (including differing perspectives of pertinent theories and concepts) and the other which reviews and critiques relevant empirical research studies and shows how these provide a niche and lead into your own work. For example, if conducting research into how children learn to read, in the first part of the review, one would review and critique the competing theories on children's literacy acquisition and learning and in the second part, empirical research studies which have investigated the topic would be discussed, focusing on the different methodologies and findings. You would then be able to show how your own research relates to and extends this work.

It may be helpful to visualise the structure of your review as a picture or diagram. Wellington et al. (2005: 82) use some diagrams to illustrate the possible ways of organising your use of the related literature (see Figure 6.2).

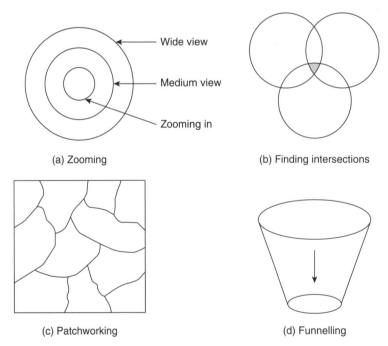

FIGURE 6.2   Organisational patterns for the literature review
Source: Wellington et al., 2005: 82

Based on these ideas, you may find it useful to devise your own picture or pictures to represent how you structure your review. You might draw a patchwork for the whole review, labelling each patch according to the different strands of your review, and devise other diagrams for each section. For example, for one theme in your review, you might choose to adopt a general to specific pattern moving from long shots to close-ups, in which case the funnelling or zooming diagrams would be suitable.

Example 6.2 Sample structure of a literature review from International Business and Management

The following example is from an MSc dissertation in the field of International Business and Management and provides an illustration of Weissberg and Buker's (1990) third approach to organising a review. The research consists of a case study which investigates the process of internationalisation and expansion for a company when entering an overseas market. The literature review explored the theory behind this process, breaking it down into four phases: pre-entry (2.2.–2.4), entry (2.5), growth and repositioning (2.6). Thus, from the contents page of the dissertation, we can see the following structure.

2.0 Literature Review

2.1 Literature Synopsis

2.2 Motives behind Internationalization

2.3 Choosing the Right Market

2.4 Deciding on When to Enter the Potential Market(s)

2.5 Entry Modes

    2.5.1 Establishing Wholly Owned Subsidiaries (WOS)

    2.5.2 Joint Venture (JV) as an Entry Mode

    2.5.3 Franchising as an Entry Mode

    2.5.4 High Control vs. Low Control

2.6 Expansion within the Market

    2.6.1 Growth Strategies – Corporate Level Strategy

2.7 Research Contribution

Source: Ovcina, 2010:7

In this chapter, the researcher explores chronologically the phases of a company's entry into a new international market from pre-entry to growth and repositioning. Within each phase he compares, contrasts and critiques different authors' theories and models. This review serves as the theoretical underpinning and framework for the case study analysis of a US retail company's entry into Latin American markets.

In the literature review example above, Dino provided a theoretical overview of a process which was then used to provide a basis for exploring a case study. As explained above, it is often relevant to also include a section or sections in your review which report on related empirical studies in your field. Findings are compared and contrasted, limitations in previous studies may be highlighted and a niche for your own work is identified (See Chapter 2, Example 2.13; Example 6.6 below, section 2.2.1; Example 6.7 below, section 1.3; Chapter 8, Example 8.2a). The tabular presentation of related empirical studies shown in Chapter 4 can provide a stepping stone for this part of the review. Thus, it is helpful to think about how the different purposes of the review will be realised in different sections and how the information and arguments in each may be presented in different ways.

Developing the structure of your review

Having considered the structure or organisational pattern of your literature review, it is important to consider the process which will help you achieve this. Swales and Feak (2000: 118–24) provide a practical reading and writing task which demonstrates, first, the importance of 'creating an architecture' for the literature review and, second, a means for creating this architecture. The underpinning principle to this process is that you put together an argument and draw on your source texts to provide support for your assertions. By developing your own argument, you show that you are using the literature for your own purposes rather than being controlled by the authors whose work you have read and are citing in your own writing.

The process involves devising an outline of your argument steps which then form the basis of the architecture of your review. For each step of your argument, group together the sources that contribute to or provide support for your assertions. If you number each of your references in EndNote or the filing system that you are using for your references, you can insert the relevant numbers beside each argument step at the planning stage. You may also wish to write down the page numbers from particular references that contain the information which is relevant for supporting your argument. Table 6.1 provides a scaffold for this planning.

TABLE 6.1   The literature review architecture

Argument steps	Relevant references and page numbers

From the argument steps that you devise, you can then develop the headings and subheadings that become the framework for your review. Using tables such as the one offered in 6.1, it is recommended that you create an overall architecture for the whole review and then more detailed ones for each section. Some researchers prefer to develop a plan like this before they start writing, whereas others write first and gradually extricate a framework from their writing.

The note card system described in Chapter 4 is a useful technique for grouping together ideas from different authors which support the particular points that you wish to make. You can physically move around the significant pieces of information from your source texts that you have recorded on your note cards according to where they best fit into your argument steps. The arrangements you make with your cards can then be recorded in an 'architecture table' such as the one shown in Table 6.1 (for a worked example, see Table 6.2).

Example 6.3 Planning your literature review

This example shows how a researcher planned and developed his argument for one section of the literature review, and is from a psychology PhD thesis first cited in in Chapter 1, Example 1.6. In the extract from the contents page of this thesis shown in Chapter 1, we saw how the literature review was introduced in the first chapter and was then revisited in different places throughout the thesis, appearing before relevant research studies. The plan reproduced in Table 6.2 was created for a section of the literature review on goal-achievement which appeared at the beginning of Webb's chapter 3, before two studies investigating the influence of personal goals on goal-attainment. The literature review discusses the wide variety of goal theories which influenced the focus of the empirical studies.

(Continued)

(Continued)

TABLE 6.2 An example of the architecture of a literature review

Section title: Models of goal-achievement

Argument steps	Relevant references
Limited previous research on comparison of goal theories	Bagozzi and Kimmel, 1995; Fredricks and Dossett, 1983; Valois et al., 1988; Cacioppo and Berntson, 1995; Weinstein, 1993
Introduce 'Rubicon model': action phases (as a means of categorising goal theories): predecisional; preactional; actional	Heckhausen, 1987; Heckhausen and Gollwitzer, 1986, 1987
Predecisional action phase: theory of planned behaviour; models of goal setting	Ajzen, 1985, 1991; Sheeran, 2002; Bandura, 1977 Locke and Latham, 1990; Carver and Scheier, 1981; Hyland, 1988; Baumeister, Heatherton and Tice, 1994; Emmons and King, 1988; Hook and Higgins, 1988
Preactional phase: theory of self-regulation; implementation intentions	Bagozzi, 1992; Abelson, 1988; Latham and Locke, 1991 Gollwitzer, 1990
Actional phase: self-regulatory strength; emotion; social influences; performance feedback.	Baumeister et al., 1994; Luminet et al., 2000; Muraven and Baumeister, 2000; Baumeister et al., 1998; Webb and Sheeran, 2003 Martin and Tesser, 1988, 1996; Keltner and Gross, 1999; Lazarus, 1991; Levenson, 1994; Kuhl, 1996, 2000 Povey et al., 2000; Rutter et al., 1993; Deci and Ryan, 1985; Tauer and Harackiewicz, 1999

Source: Adapted from Webb, 2003: 50–1

In terms of a structural pattern for this section of the review, it involved a comparison of different approaches. The diagram of a patchwork from Figure 6.2 depicts it well, with each patch representing a different goal theory.

Task 6.1 Structuring your own literature review

Try the activities below in relation to your whole literature review or one or two sections of it.

1 Draw a picture which represents the structure of your own literature review.
2 Fill in a table outlining the steps of the argument that you intend to follow in your review. Give the supporting references and specific page numbers for each argument step. You will add to these references gradually and over time as your reading progresses.

The relationship between the introduction and the literature review

Another important aspect of the integration of the literature into your dissertation or thesis to consider is the relationship between the references cited in the introduction and those cited in the literature review. In some fields, such as medicine, the introduction is a long chapter which includes the literature review. However, in many other disciplines, you are likely to have a separate introduction followed by the literature review. If uncertain about the best approach to adopt, you can clarify the conventions and expectations in your field by consultation with your supervisor and by looking at previous dissertations or theses in your field.

Some of the multiple purposes of the literature review which were referred to in Chapter 2 of this book may be partially or fully realised in the introduction. These purposes are repeated here as a reminder of the variety of reasons for which we include references to the work of others in research writing.

- to provide a historical background for your research;
- to give an overview of the current context in which your research is situated by referring to contemporary debates, issues and questions in the field;
- to discuss relevant theories and concepts which underpin your research;
- to introduce relevant terminology and provide definitions to clarify how terms are being used in the context of your own work;
- to describe related research in the field and show how your work extends or challenges this, or addresses a gap in previous work in the field;
- to provide supporting evidence for a practical problem or issue which your research is addressing thereby underlining its significance.

If adopting a conventional structure for your thesis or dissertation, where in the final version of the paper you have an introduction that is followed by one or more chapters which constitute the literature review, there will be references to sources of information and related research in both these parts. As suggested above, it can sometimes be difficult to decide which references to include in the introduction and which ones to refer to in the literature review. Researchers make individual decisions about how to organise the information in these two parts of the dissertation or thesis. Nevertheless, there are some general principles regarding which purposes are likely to be fulfilled in the different chapters. The discussion below offers suggestions which will help you decide how to differentiate between the content you decide to include in these initial chapters.

The introduction is usually relatively brief compared with the literature review. An approximate guideline to bear in mind is that the introduction should be about 10 per cent of the whole dissertation or thesis and the literature review 20 per cent (Barnes, 1995 cited in Blaxter et al., 2010).

In the introduction, it is common practice to provide:

- a brief historical and/or contemporary context for the research;
- a concise reference to research already carried out in the field;
- an outline of the research problem that needs to be explored as a result of a gap left by previous research or an issue that needs resolving;
- a justification for the proposed research;
- an outline of the contents of the different chapters in the dissertation or thesis.

Some of these purposes will be revisited more comprehensively in the literature review. For example, you may expand on the historical and contemporary context in which your work is situated. You are also likely to identify and discuss the key theories, concepts and terminology which are relevant to your research topic and explore these in sufficient depth for the type and level of research that you are undertaking. Additionally, you will probably *explore* in more detail related empirical research studies in the field and once again highlight how your work extends that of others or fills a gap. Examples 6.4–6.7 included below show how different researchers have developed an organisational structure for their literature review. They illustrate how the categories for the reading led into argument steps and section headings in the literature reviews. The extracts also show how each of the researchers gives an overview of the structure of the literature review in the introduction of the chapter to signal to the reader how the argument will be presented.

Example 6.4 Reading, planning and signposting the structure of the review

For her masters dissertation in town and regional planning, Emma conducted research into the range of influences on planning decisions in urban settings. She was interested in the role universal values have in planning decisions, in particular those decisions which are concerned with conservation and regeneration issues. Her research focus was on how the various stakeholders in the process are conditioned by different values. She analysed this in the context of two case studies.

eg → To make the reading manageable, she broke it down under the following headings.

1 The role of 'values' in planning research
2 Stakeholders in planning decisions
3 Universal values in relation to planning

4   Particularity of place in planning decisions
5   Participatory planning
6   Conservation in urban settings
7   Regeneration in urban settings

This resulted in the following framework or 'architecture' for her literature review which appears as Chapter 2 after the introduction of her dissertation. The headings which appear on the contents page are shown below.

2.0   Literature Review: introduction
2.1   The importance of value
2.3   The public interest and stakeholder relations
2.4   The universal and the particular
2.5   The value of conservation and regeneration in historic urban quarters
2.6   Implications for conservation/regeneration initiatives: the case studies

Source: Adapted from Coveney, 2003: i

The connections can be seen again with the introductory paragraph of her review which outlines how she is going to discuss the literature which underpins her research.

eg →   As stated in the introduction, this study is about values in planning and uses the relationship between conservation and regeneration in historic urban quarters as an illustration. This chapter introduces the 'values approach' to planning, looking firstly at why questions of value are so important. It then considers three notions fundamental to the approach in more depth: those of the public interest and stakeholder relations, the relationship between the universal and the particular, and finally the implications for participatory planning. The final part of this chapter considers the relationship between the practices of conservation and regeneration and the values surrounding them and explains the choice of the case studies.

Source: Adapted from Coveney, 2003: 5

Example 6.5 Signposting and structuring the review

In her PhD thesis on Education for sustainable development, Ling outlines the organisational structure of her literature review in two different places: in the Introduction, Section 1.4,

(Continued)

(Continued)

'Outline of the thesis', and in Section 2.1, which is the introduction of her literature review (see Table of contents of full thesis in Chapter 1, Example 1.4). I include the paragraph from the beginning of her literature review (Section 2.1) below.

 The main body of this review consists of five sections. To set the scene for and to provide contextualising information about the research topic, I critically review the notion of SD (section 2.2), and the history of sustainability education (section 2.3). I move on to discuss four key curriculum perspectives – technical, socially-critical, liberal-progressive and postmodern perspectives – and their relevance to sustainability education (section 2.4). Amongst the four perspectives, I focus on the last three as the theoretical framework of the research. Finally, I introduce English and Chinese HE and their respective responses to sustainability education, their differences and similarities (section 2.5) as well as issues involved in learning across national and cultural boundaries (section 2.6).

Source: Feng, 2010: 14–15

To focus more specifically on one part of the literature review chapter, we shall now turn to Section 2.2. In preparation for this part, where the concept of sustainable development is explored and critiqued, Ling organised her reading into the following areas. These themes later led to her choice of the subheadings for the Section.

Sustainable development: origins and ongoing issues (2.2)

Interpretations of 'sustainable' (2.2.1)

Interpretations of 'development' (2.2.1)

Sustainable development and capitalism (2.2.2)

Intragenerational equity: developing countries and climate change (2.2.3)

Anthropocentrism and ecocentrism (2.2.4)

Overall complexity and uncertainty of the concept of sustainable development (2.2.5)

Positive and encouraging examples which support the potential of sustainable development (2.2.6 and 2.2.7)

The subheadings below show how Ling organised her critique in the thesis. Sections 2.2.1—2.2.5 raise a number of challenges to the concept of sustainable development and then in Sections 2.2.6 and 2.2.7 she argues how specific international conferences, documents and events offer hope for overcoming some of these and thus support sustainable development.

2.2 The notion of sustainable development (SD)

  2.2.1 Oxymoron?

  2.2.2 Business as usual

2.2.3 Intragenerational equity

2.2.4 Anthropocentrism versus ecocentrism

2.2.5 Complexity and uncertainty

2.2.6 A way forward

2.2.7 Changes occurring

Source: Feng, 2010: i

Examples 6.6 and 6.7 below illustrate the choices different researchers have made with regard to way they have used the related literature in the introduction and the literature review. No hard and fast rules exist with regard to what is covered in each part of the dissertation or thesis, but from these two examples we can see how two more researchers have organised their content to fulfil all the necessary purposes of using the literature for their particular piece of research.

Example 6.6 The introduction and the literature review

This example is taken from doctoral research which investigated information management among health visitors in the UK. Extracts in Example 6.6 are adapted from Bacigalupo (2000).

The title

The Information Management of Health Visitors: with particular reference to their public health and community development activities

The research questions

How can the way that health visitors deal with information in public health and community development settings be understood in relation to the health service context and current information management concepts and processes?

What are the implications of that understanding in terms of developing recommendations and guidelines for practice?

(Continued)

(Continued)

Reading categories

The researcher developed the following categories for her reading:

Information management

History

Concepts

Processes

Previous research

User studies

Information needs

Information seeking behaviour

Information audit (methodology for assessing needs)

Information management in the NHS

Strategies

Problems

Achievements

Needs and resources

Public health

Health visiting

Community development work

Government policy and legislation in public health

This led into the following structure for the first three chapters of the PhD thesis.

The contents page

Chapter 1 Introduction (pp. 3–9)

1.1 The motive for the research

1.2 The research questions

1.3 The current context

    1.3.1 Changes in the UK National Health Service

    1.3.2 Changes in UK government policy: a focus on the community

    1.3.3 NHS policy: maximizing the potential of IT

Source: Bacigalupo, 2000: i

In terms of the purposes served by the references to the literature, the different chapters cover the following. The introduction outlines the current context in relation to the National Health Service, information management, and government policy; states the research questions and research focus; justifies the research; and provides a definition of information management. At the end of this chapter, an outline of the content of each of the chapters of the thesis is given.

Chapter 2 outlines the historical context of information management and information management in the NHS; introduces concepts and terminology relevant for the field; and shows how the current research addresses a gap in existing research. Chapter 3 gives more detail of the historical and current context within the field of public health.

(Continued)

(Continued)

The conclusion to Chapter 2 is included below. The phrases used give an example of how the researcher signals what she is doing in relation to the literature in the different chapters of her thesis.

Summary of chapter 2

 This chapter has discussed information management concepts in general and recent developments with regard to information management in the NHS. The need for information management research into how health visitors deal with information has been highlighted. The next chapter reviews the literature regarding the public health and community development activities of health visitors in order to show that this area is particularly relevant for research.

Source: Bacigalupo, 2000: 39

Example 6.7 The introduction and the literature review

The study here was for a masters dissertation and looked at the effect of instruction on two aspects of EFL (English as a foreign language) learners' pronunciation: the production of specific features of pronunciation and general intelligibility. Extracts in example 6.5 are adapted from Moore (2001), referred to in earlier chapters.

The title

The Effects of Formal Instruction on EFL Pronunciation Acquisition: A Case Study from Germany

The hypotheses

H0 = a course of pronunciation instruction does not improve a learner's production of specific features of pronunciation.

H1 = a course of pronunciation instruction improves a learner's production of specific features of pronunciation.

H0 = a course of pronunciation instruction does not improve a learner's general intelligibility.

H1 = a course of pronunciation instruction improves a learner's general intelligibility.

Categories for reading

Features of pronunciation and 'intelligibility'

Second language learning and acquisition

Second language instruction

Pronunciation instruction

Other factors that influence effective pronunciation

The architecture of the first three chapters of the dissertation, which was developed from the reading, is shown in the following extract from the contents page.

The contents page

Introduction

Justification for the research

The context: the English Language Teaching Institution and the learners

Outline of the dissertation

Chapter 1 Literature review

1.1 Historical Background

1.2 Target Pronunciation and Intelligibility

1.3 Research into the Effects of Instruction

 1.3.1 Second Language Research

 1.3.2 Pronunciation Research

1.4 Specific Features of Pronunciation

 1.4.1 Strong and Weak Forms of words

 1.4.2 Contractions and Elision

 1.4.3 Assimilation

 1.4.4 Liaison

 1.4.5 Stress

 1.4.6 Intonation

1.5 Summary

Chapter 2 The experiment

2.1 Aims and rationale of the experiment: the hypotheses

Source: Moore, 2001: iii

(Continued)

(Continued)

In terms of the purposes served by the references to the literature, the different chapters cover the following. The introduction introduces the topic of pronunciation; provides a justification for the research; outlines the current context of the research; and gives an outline of the content of each chapter in the dissertation.

The literature review (Chapter 1) provides a historical context, describes related research which shows how current research is filling a gap and extending work that has been done before; and defines relevant terms for the field of research. The hypotheses are given at the beginning of Chapter 2.

The final paragraph of the introduction is included below to show the way in which the researcher signals how the literature is integrated into the dissertation.

eg → Having briefly outlined the rationale behind the study, the first chapter will review the pertinent literature on the effects of instruction both on second language learning in general and also specifically on pronunciation. Other factors involved in the learning process will also be considered since second language acquisition is a highly complex process. By considering the research in the field, a general framework will be provided for this study and the discussion presented in the second chapter. Finally, the first chapter will present an outline of the specific features of pronunciation under consideration in this study. The second chapter will describe the experiment that was conducted to investigate the effects of instruction on pronunciation and present the data analysis and a discussion of the results. In the final chapter, the constraints of this study will be discussed, followed by implications for further research.

Source: Moore, 2001: 2

Task 6.2 Reflecting on your own research field

Ask your supervisor to recommend a thesis or dissertation in your field. Look carefully at the contents page and identify whether a distinct chapter or chapters constitute the literature review. Read the introduction and the literature review chapter/s. Identify the purposes for which the researcher is using the related literature. Note, in particular, the way the various purposes are realised in either the introduction and/or the literature review.

Summary

To summarise, this chapter has considered:

- the cyclical, continuous, and interconnected nature of the various processes involved in the literature review;
- techniques for starting to write about the relevant literature of your field;
- the various structures that might be adopted for the literature review or for different parts of it;
- the relationship between the introduction and the literature review;
- some examples from dissertations and theses which show how different researchers have organised their use of the literature.

7

In-text citations

Chapter summary

This chapter discusses:

- the reasons for in-text referencing;
- plagiarism and the various ways that it can occur;
- the type of information that requires a reference;
- the different referencing systems and their formats;
- integral and non-integral references and the possible reasons for using each style;
- summarising, paraphrasing, generalisations, and direct quotations;
- the range of reporting verbs and tense differences;
- disciplinary difference in relation to citation choices.

In academic writing, it is important to include references to the work of others in two places in your document: first, within the main body of the text and, second, in a bibliography or list of references at the end of the document (see Chapter 5). References within the main body of the text are known as 'in-text citations' and this chapter focuses on the variety of ways in which they can be presented. The three terms 'reference', 'citation' and 'acknowledgement' are all used synonymously in this chapter to mean the explicit mention of a source from where information is taken.

Citations, or references to other authors, within the main body of the text of a dissertation or thesis occur when propositional content is attributed to another source (Hyland, 2004). This important academic convention demonstrates the interactive nature of research writing; by referencing authors in your field you are entering into a written dialogue with others and therefore beginning to participate in a research community.

Why do we reference?

An understanding of the reasons why citations are included in research writing can help you to recognise the importance of adopting the expected conventions of your university and department. It also helps you to identify the situations in which you need to provide a reference. Although there are differences of opinion among academics about the predominant reasons for citations, and indeed these may vary depending on the level of study and the discipline, we can summarise the main purposes as follows. Your in-text references show that you are:

- acknowledging and showing respect for other researchers' contributions to the field;
- demonstrating your allegiance to a particular research community;
- establishing your own credibility by the location of your work within a particular field;
- providing justification and support for your assertions and arguments;
- giving an illustration of how you have developed your argument;
- creating a niche for your own research by showing how you wish to extend or challenge previous studies;
- comparing, contrasting and evaluating the work others have done in the field;
- illustrating your own understanding of the subject matter by demonstrating that you have read widely and are able to select relevant information to contextualise your own research;
- enabling readers to track down your source texts easily if they wish to find out more information;
- allowing the accuracy of your work to be checked;
- avoiding plagiarism.

What is plagiarism?

Plagiarism has been considered in the context of note taking (see Chapter 4). It was emphasised that taking effective notes from a source text encourages you to use your own words when you paraphrase or summarise that information in your writing. It is important to do this because one very common form of plagiarism is the use of the same or similar words to the original text; this is plagiarism even if the source author is acknowledged.

Here we extend the discussion to examine the other ways that plagiarism can occur and give some examples. If you conduct a Google search for 'definition of plagiarism' you find a host of web sites where the term is defined by different institutions and dictionaries. The following is a commonly recognised interpretation:

> **Plagiarism** is the deliberate or unintentional use of the ideas, words or work of others without acknowledgement; it occurs when an individual, whether knowingly or unknowingly, presents something as their own when in fact it has come from someone else's work and the source has not been appropriately referenced.

The descriptions below outline more specifically the main ways in which plagiarism can occur. It is essential to recognise that any of these can occur either intentionally and unintentionally; hence all of the situations described below would constitute plagiarism even if the writer has not deliberately been dishonest and has simply misunderstood that these actions come under the umbrella of plagiarism:

- the wholesale copying of another's work and claiming it as your own; for example, it is plagiarism if you download a dissertation from the Internet and then copy and submit some or all of it as your work. This would be the most blatant and dishonest form of plagiarism.
- Rephrasing someone else's original ideas and not acknowledging the source: unless it is information which is recognised as common knowledge, even when rephrasing the source material into your own words, it must be referenced. Students sometimes worry that they may write or produce something themselves and not realise that someone else has said this before. There are no easy answers to this scenario but by conducting comprehensive literature searches you should be able to identify who has previously done work which is close to your own in the field and reference accordingly.
- Using material which is recognised as common knowledge in your field but copying the information word for word from a text book. The ideas do not require a reference if considered to be common knowledge but it is still plagiarism to copy from a textbook verbatim.
- Acknowledging the source but using the exact wording of the original or wording that is very close to the original; although you can use a cited author's exact words if making a direct quotation, you should only use direct quotations selectively. As mentioned in Chapter 4, an overdependence on direct quotations masks the writer's own understanding and interpretation of the area that is being discussed.
- Self-plagiarism; a student should not submit the same piece of work verbatim for two different assessments. It is acceptable to reference a previous assignment using the standard conventions. In some circumstances, it may be appropriate to repurpose the assignment by restructuring, extending or reducing it for a subsequent piece of work, but the exact wording should be changed. For example, you may have been required to write a research proposal in one module which included a literature review and an account of your research methodology. Undoubtedly, parts of this will be extended and

presented in a slightly different way in the subsequent research dissertation. If adapted in this way, it would not be self-plagiarism.

- Copying and pasting from the Internet into your own work; any copying and pasting from web sites, however small a section, constitutes plagiarism if not correctly referenced. If it is common knowledge, the information should be rephrased into your own words. The principles surrounding the use of material from the Internet are the same as those for printed sources and the same conventions of acknowledgement should be followed.

The two additional practices below constitute a grey area which often occurs when students are in the process of learning the commonly recognised conventions of academic writing and the referencing practices which are seen as acceptable.

- Patchworking (Hull and Rose 1989; Howard 1995): this occurs when a writer takes sentences from a number of different sources on a related theme and 'patchworks' them together. The different sentences all may be referenced using appropriate conventions but the wording of each one is very similar to the original source. Whilst it is good practice to be integrating material from a variety of places, it must be reworded as well as acknowledged.
- Over dependence on direct quotations; this arises when an author uses a number of direct quotations from different sources, all of which may be correctly set out with quotation marks, appropriate citations and page numbers. However, if the number of direct quotations is excessive, there is not enough evidence of the writer's own words or interpretation. More paraphrasing and summarising with appropriate acknowledgement and the writer's own linking sentences must be included.

The important message underlying all these definitions is that the source of the ideas that you use must be acknowledged according to the particular conventions of your institution and your discipline. If the referencing conventions are followed carefully, plagiarism is unlikely to occur. It can, however, sometimes be difficult to identify and fully comprehend the expected conventions and put them into practice. The guidelines below give an overview of the different formats and styles that are currently used for citations, and the functions and situations in which they are appropriate. At the end of the chapter, there are some examples of acceptable and unacceptable borrowing from source texts. There is also a description of an online resource called Turnitin which enables you to find out the extent to which your writing has used others' words. But first of all, we consider the type of information for which it is necessary to provide a reference and the variety of formats for in-text references. It is important as well to remember copyright legislation and the need to seek a copyright holder's permission (see Chapter 5) if making extensive use of copied illustrations, maps, or diagrams from a specific source in your dissertation or thesis.

What type of information requires a reference?

The general rule to bear in mind is that you do not need a reference for information that is considered to be common knowledge and is in the public domain. Typically, this is information that is generally accepted as being true – a fact – in your field.

On the other hand, the origin of an idea or an opinion, research finding or theory that is open to challenge and debate should be referenced. This category would include statistics, formulae and illustrations. In some disciplines, especially where the development of knowledge tends to be cumulative, information which once required a reference can become common knowledge over time. For example, although it was once contested that the earth was round, we can now safely assume that this is a commonly accepted fact which does not need to be referenced. However, in other disciplines such as philosophy, where knowledge is constantly being debated, reinterpreted and revisited, the concept of 'common knowledge' is more remote. Indeed, research has shown that the number of citations used in the humanities and social sciences is far greater than in science and engineering (Hyland, 2004).

The two statements about Christopher Columbus in Example 7.1 illustrate the difference between common and contested knowledge. In the first example, no citation is included as it is widely accepted that Columbus did undertake the voyage across the Atlantic in 1492. However, the second statement does require a source to be given as the location of the remains of Columbus is still disputed.

Example 7.1 Common or contested knowledge

Christopher Columbus sailed across the Atlantic Ocean in 1492.

According to recent research involving DNA samples from 500-year-old bones, it has been claimed that Christopher Columbus is buried in the cathedral in Seville, Spain and not in the Dominican Republic. (Associated Press, 2006).

Sometimes, there can be a difference of opinion about whether a piece of information is common knowledge or not. Indeed, a clear distinction between a contestable idea and a commonly agreed fact is not always possible. If you are in any doubt about whether a piece of information requires a citation, it is a good idea to provide one to avoid any risk of plagiarism.

Referencing systems

There are three main systems for referencing. Table 7.1 shows these different formats and the corresponding layout of the bibliography or list of references at the end of the dissertation or thesis. There is usually an accepted system in your discipline so it is a good idea to consult any departmental guidelines you can find. Alternatively, you can look in an important journal in your field and follow the system that it requires for the articles it publishes.

As indicated in Table 7.1, the format of the reference may vary according to the conventions of your discipline. If following the Harvard system, the reference includes the surname of the cited author and the year of publication of the work cited. If the reference is a direct quotation, the page number should also be included. Alternatively, a numerical system of referencing may be used in some science and engineering fields. When a citation occurs within the text, a full sized number is used in brackets which corresponds to the number allocated to the full reference in the bibliography. The use of a numerical system does not preclude the use of an author's name as part of a sentence in the main body of the text but, because in the fields in which this system is used it is more conventional to foreground the research and the findings as opposed to the researchers who conduct the work, the use of author names is not usual or frequent.

Whichever formatting system you adopt, there are a number of different ways that the work of others can be presented in your writing. The range of possibilities is outlined below.

TABLE 7.1   In-text referencing systems and the bibliography

In-text referencing style	Sequence of entries in the 'List of references' or 'Bibliography'
Harvard system: Author surname (or occasionally, first name and surname) and year of publication of the work cited. (This is the most widely used format across a wide range of disciplines.)	Alphabetical list of references according to author surnames.
Numerical system: A full size number is used after the referenced information in the text. (This system is more common in science and engineering disciplines.)	Numerical list of references corresponding to the order in which each reference first appears in the main body of text in the dissertation or thesis.
Footnotes or endnotes: A small superscript number is used after the referenced information in the text; the full reference is given at the bottom of the page in a footnote or at the end of the chapter in an endnote. (This system is more common in disciplines such as English literature.)	Alphabetical list of references according to author surnames.

Integral and non-integral references

The first important distinction to be made is between integral and non-integral references, and the impact of disciplinary convention on their use.

Integral references

An integral reference is a citation where the cited author's name has a grammatical function in the sentence in which you include it in your writing. There are various ways in which an integral reference can occur. First, the cited author can be the subject of a sentence which includes a paraphrase, summary or direct quotation from the cited author's work (see Example 7.2).

Example 7.2 Cited author as subject

Donna Haraway (1991, 1997), amongst other scholars, has argued that knowledge is embodied and situated, that the content of a scientific text is shaped by the place of its production.

Source: Meyer, 2006: 8.

Second, the cited author can be included in an adjunct phrase at the beginning of the sentence (see Example 7.3).

Example 7.3 Cited author in initial adjunct phrase

According to Barone et al. (1997), it is part of the current agenda of social cognitive psychology to acquire a better understanding of individual differences in self-regulation.

Source: Woodgate, 2005: 4

Third, the cited author can be the agent of the verb in a passive sentence and follows the preposition 'by', as in Example 7.4.

Example 7.4 Cited author as agent in passive sentence

One cross-sectional study that may support this hypothesis was conducted by Gyurcsik and Brawley (2001).

Source: Woodgate, 2005: 34

Integral references are often more suitable if you wish to emphasise the cited author's ownership of the ideas being cited. By the selective use of reporting verbs such as 'argues', 'believes' and 'found', it is possible to indicate the attitude or strength of commitment of the cited author to the piece of information being cited. You can also give an indication of your own view of the cited information by your choice (see section below on 'Choice of reporting verb' and Chapter 9). For example, by using a reported verb such as 'argue' you can show that the information you are incorporating is the opinion of the cited author and that you or others might not agree. In fields such as the humanities and the social sciences where knowledge is more fluid and contested, a writer is likely to make more frequent use of reporting verbs.

Example 7.5 shows how the writer uses integral references to illustrate the views of three different authors (or groups of authors) in relation to the

Example 7.5 Integral references for a comparison of viewpoints

According to Milroy and Milroy (1997: 52), language maintenance (LM) can signify the 'process of consciously maintaining – if necessary by government intervention – a particular form of a language in a population where there is linguistic diversity ...' or it can refer to non-institutional practice in small-scale communities to ensure the survival of the community language. Thieberger (1992: 334) views LM as either (i) a description of the state of shift that a language has undergone (that is, how much of a language is actually maintained) or (ii) those activities engaged in with an aim of maintaining languages. For Fase et al. (1992), LM refers to keeping the language in use as well as maintaining the users' proficiency in the language. For the purpose of this study, LM can be viewed as ...

Source: Lee, 2003: 52–3

definition of the term, 'language maintenance'. She clearly emphasises the three sources and the alternative definitions and then moves on to specify how her own research uses the term.

Non-integral references

In a non-integral reference the cited author's name appears in brackets outside the structure of the sentence in the text and has no grammatical function within that sentence. If using a numerical system of referencing, a number appears in brackets after the referenced information. Examples 7.6, 7.7 and 7.8 show various ways non-integral references can be used. The first is a single reference.

Example 7.6 A single non-integral reference

eg →

There are four broad categories of issues that affect commitment: personal characteristics, role-related characteristics, structural characteristics, and work experiences (Mowday et al. 1982).

Source: Culverson, 2002: 27

The second type of non-integral reference is a piece of information attributed to more than one source – a generalisation.

Example 7.7 A generalisation: combined attribution

eg →

Role-related characteristics of organizational commitment are also discussed in terms of job scope or challenge, role conflict, and role ambiguity (Mowday et al., 1982; Allen and Meyer, 1990).

Source: Culverson, 2002: 32

Example 7.8 illustrates a sequence of non-integral references with a range of findings or viewpoints being attributed to different authors.

**Example 7.8 Attribution
to different authors**

Other notable effects [of organizational change] include reduced job satisfaction and distrust (Bateman and Strasser, 1984), a decline in motivation (Mowday, Porter and Steers, 1982; Bennett and Durkin, 2000), absenteeism (Mowday et al., 1982; Clegg, 1983), health (Begley and Czajka, 1993), union issues and job insecurity (Worral et al., 2000).

Source: Culverson, 2002: 16–17

The use of a non-integral reference is a way of emphasising the idea, theory or finding rather than the person who is being attributed with saying it. The three examples of non-integral references provided all illustrate the way the source information is brought into the foreground rather than the cited author. This technique also enables the writer of the thesis or dissertation to give the impression that he or she is in control of the content being cited (see Chapter 9). The writer is using the source material to structure and support his or her own argument and by acknowledging the author in a non-integral reference he or she is reducing the risk of the text being dominated by the cited authors. Sometimes, the use of non-integral references can create confusion as it may not be clear how much of the preceding text should be attributed to the author being cited. In Example 7.8, we can see how the writer carefully attributes each idea to a specific author or authors, thus avoiding any confusion.

Disciplinary difference in reference type

There are disciplinary differences in the use of integral and non-integral references. Research conducted by Ken Hyland (2004) provides some useful statistics to illustrate this point. He examined citation practices in 80 published journal articles from eight different disciplines. One article was taken from ten leading journals in each of the eight fields. The percentages of integral and non-integral references in the journal articles from the different disciplines are shown in Table 7.2. These statistics suggest that in all disciplines, with the exception of philosophy, non-integral references are more common. Overall, the percentages of non-integral citations are higher in the science and engineering disciplines than in the social sciences and humanities. Of course, it is important to note that this research was based on journal articles and not doctoral theses or masters dissertations. However, the findings give an indication of the ways that established authors in academic disciplines integrate source material into their writing, thus showing the conventions which tend to be adhered to in the field.

TABLE 7.2   Integral and non-integral references in different disciplines

Discipline	Non-integral (%)	Integral (%)
Biology	90.2	9.8
Electronic engineering	84.3	15.7
Physics	83.1	16.9
Mechanical engineering	71.3	28.7
Marketing	70.3	29.7
Applied linguistics	65.6	34.4
Sociology	64.6	35.4
Philosophy	35.4	64.6

Source: Hyland, 2004: 24. Reprinted with permission from Ken Hyland, *Disciplinary Discourses: Social Interactions in Academic Writing,* The University of Michigan Press © 2004.

Types of citation

The four main citation patterns

As well as the distinction between integral and non-integral references, it is also important to stress that there are different types of citation – a summary, a generalisation, and a short or long direct quotation – all of which can be presented in the text with either an integral or non-integral reference. Examples of these four main patterns are given in Examples 7.9 to 7.12.

In Example 7.9 the writer has summarised in his own words a piece of information from Wegner and Wheatley, in this case, with an integral reference.

Example 7.9 A Summary

... several research programs have challenged the assumption that intentions are an important cause of behaviour. For example, Wegner and Wheatley (1999) proposed that the subjective experience of intentions causing behaviour is an illusion.

Source: Webb, 2003: 18

Also see Examples 7.2 to 7.6 above.

In Example 7.10 the writer has summarised in his own words information about a field of research which is attributed to different groups of researchers. Two extracts are given below in Example 7.10. The first example of generalisation is interesting because the reference to Bargh and colleagues appears as both an integral and a non-integral reference.

Example 7.10 Generalisation:
combined attribution

Wegner and Wheatley pointed to an influential program of research by Bargh and colleagues (e.g., Bargh and Chartrand, 1999; Bargh, Chen, and Burrows, 1996; Bargh and Ferguson, 2000; Bargh, et al., 2001) which suggests that behaviour is determined by mental processes that are put into motion by features of the environment and that operate outside of conscious awareness and guidance. In sum, whereas several models of health and social behaviour assume that intentions cause behaviour, recent research into automatic behaviour and the illusion of conscious posits little or no causal role for intention.

Source: Webb, 2003: 18

The unitization hypothesis (Healy and Drenowski, 1983; Healy, Oliver and McNamara, 1987) argues that rapid perception of the word as a unit interferes with the perception of its components.

Source: Webb, 2003: 119

Also see Example 7.7 above.

It is less common for a combined attribution to be introduced by an integral reference because, when making a generalisation in this way, the intention is usually to emphasise the cited information as opposed to the cited authors. It is also more reader-friendly to group a sequence of authors' names in brackets outside the structure of the sentence as a list of authors' names within a sentence in a text tends to be distracting.

In Example 7.11, the writer has quoted the exact words from the source text and placed them within quotation marks. Because the quotation is short, it has been embedded within the text. The first part of the citation shown below is, in fact, a paraphrase or summary of information from the source text and the direct quotation comprises only a small number of the exact words of the original. A page number is mentioned because it is a direct quotation.

Example 7.11 A short direct quotation

Wegner and Wheatley (1999) proposed that the subjective experience of intentions causing behaviour is an illusion; both intention and behaviour are caused by a third variable; 'unconscious mechanisms of the mind' (490).

Source: Webb, 2003: 18

The fourth main citation type is a long direct quotation (see Example 7.12). Because the quotation is long (more than two lines) it is indented, single spaced and separated from the main text. A page number is included because it is a direct quotation using the exact words of the original. In most disciplines if you

Example 7.12 A long direct quotation

... Muraven et al. (1998) suggest that:

> It is good to exert self-control on a regular basis because in the long run, these exercises will strengthen self-control and make a person less susceptible to the depleting effects of a single exertion. (456)

Source: Webb, 2003: 88–9

separate and single space a long quote from the main body of the text in this way, you do not need quotation marks to indicate it is a direct quotation.

It is recommended that you check the conventions and expectations of your discipline with respect to the maximum length of quotations that may run on in the main body of the text and the precise layout of longer quotations which are separated from the main text. Because it is important that direct quotations should be particularly pertinent to the topic under discussion, you can make use of ellipsis marks ... to show that you have omitted words from the original source, and parentheses ( ) or brackets [ ] to show you are adding words which ensure the direct quote blends with your own text smoothly.

Disciplinary difference in citation type

Drawing again on the research cited from Hyland (2004), we can observe disciplinary difference in the use of the four main citation patterns. Table 7.3 shows the percentages of each type of citation pattern in each of the disciplines in Hyland's study.

Interestingly, Hyland's figures show that quotations do not appear at all in the journal articles from science and engineering fields. In addition, even though they are more common in the humanities and the social sciences, there are a far greater number of summaries and generalisations. A direct quotation tends to be used only when the cited author makes a point in particularly effective words. Quotes are generally used sparingly and do not provide a cover for long stretches of text which are difficult to paraphrase. If overused, extracts give the impression that the author has not fully understood the material they are citing/quoting. Thus, it is a more common practice across all disciplines to acknowledge the source and put the cited information into your own words. Generalisations (combined attributions) are less common than summaries in all fields, and notably less so in philosophy.

TABLE 7.3 Citation types in different disciplines

Discipline	Quote (%)	Block quote (%)	Summary (%)	Generalisation (%)
Biology	0	0	72	38
Electronic engineering	0	0	66	34
Physics	0	0	68	32
Mechanical engineering	0	0	67	33
Marketing	3	2	68	27
Applied linguistics	8	2	67	23
Sociology	8	5	69	18
Philosophy	2	1	89	8

Source: Hyland, 2004: 26. Reprinted with permission from Ken Hyland, *Disciplinary Discourses: Social Interactions in Academic Writing,* The University of Michigan Press © 2004.

Choice of reporting verb

A further choice to be made with regard to citations is that of the reporting verb and its tense. If using an integral reference, a reporting verb is often necessary. It introduces what the cited author thinks, said or did. In Example 7.13 'argued' is the reporting verb.

Example 7.13 The reporting verb

Ambrose (1991: 86) argued that the policy of containment acted as a guiding light for the United States to emerge from isolationism and make a strong commitment to intervention in global affairs for the first time 'in a period of general peace'.

Source: Son, 2004: 16

Reporting verbs can be categorised according to the type of activity they represent on the part of the cited author (Thomas and Hawes, 1994; Thompson and Ye, 1991):

- 'Doing' activities refer to procedures and research findings, for example: *observe, discover, show, illustrate, analyse, conduct, study, examine.*
- 'Thinking' activities refer to an author's beliefs and thoughts, for example: *believe, view, speculate.*
- 'Discussion' activities refer to what a cited author has said, for example: *argue, discuss, suggest, state, propose, claim, describe.*

Disciplinary difference in reporting verbs

Hyland's research shows us which reporting verbs are most common in the research articles from the disciplines included in his study (Hyland, 2004). From his findings, it appears that verbs which represent 'doing' activities are the most commonly chosen reporting verbs in science and engineering, whereas in the humanities and social sciences the reporting verbs denoting 'thinking' and 'discussion' activities are more frequently selected (see Table 7.4).

The evaluative function of reporting verbs is explored in Chapter 9, where there is also further discussion of the reasons why certain reporting verbs,

TABLE 7.4   The most frequently used reporting verbs in different disciplines

Discipline	Most frequent forms of reporting verb
Philosophy	say, suggest, argue, claim, point out, propose, think
Sociology	argue, suggest, describe, note, analyse, discuss
Applied linguistics	suggest, argue, show, explain, find, point out
Marketing	suggest, argue, demonstrate, propose, show
Biology	describe, find, report, show, suggest, observe
Electronic engineering	propose, use, describe, show, publish
Mechanical engineering	describe, show, report, discuss
Physics	develop, report, study

Source: Hyland, 2004: 27. Reprinted with permission from Ken Hyland, *Disciplinary Discourses: Social Interactions in Academic Writing,* The University of Michigan Press © 2004.

such as 'argue' and 'suggest', are more common in the humanities and social sciences than in science and engineering.

Tense of reporting verb

Another decision that a writer must take when using reporting verbs is the choice of verb tense. It will probably not be until completing later drafts that you will want to focus in detail on the issues outlined in this section but it is helpful to have an overview of tense usage when reporting the work of others from an early stage. There are three main tenses that you can choose between:

- the past simple tense – Hall (2006) explained how …
- the present perfect tense – Hall (2006) has explained how …
- the present simple tense – Hall (2006) explains how …

These will be discussed and illustrated in the following three subsections. (Italicising of the verbs is my emphasis.)

The past simple tense

The past simple is the safest tense to choose for a reporting verb as, in the majority of circumstances, it is grammatically acceptable. In particular, when referring to what a researcher did, the past simple is more common for the reporting verb because the action represented by the verb refers to an activity which took place at a specific moment in the past.

Example 7.14 Reporting verb in the past simple

Chappelle et al. (1995) *found* that the intermediate species hydrogen was potentially important for diagnosing which anaerobic respiration process was dominant.

Source: Watson, 2004: 12

The present perfect tense

The present perfect is common when referring to an area of enquiry within which a number of researchers are working. Example 7.15 provides an illustration.

Example 7.15 Verb in the present perfect

Reactive transport modelling of groundwater systems *has become* an important field of research during recent years (e.g. Zheng and Bennett, 1995; Steefel and MacQuarrie, 1996...)

Source: Watson, 2004: 12

In Example 7.16 the general area of research is referred to using the present perfect ('have also considered') and then the past simple is used when a specific piece of research is mentioned ('investigated').

Example 7.16 Contrast between the present perfect and the past simple.

Numerous experiments *have also considered* the efficiency of action initiation as a function of implementation intentions. For example, Webb and Sheeran (2003) *investigated* the relationship between implementation intentions and ego-depletion.

Source: Webb, 2003: 14

The present simple tense

While reading around your topic you have probably noticed that it is common for authors to use the present tense when reporting what a cited author thinks, believes, writes, or says. The move from past to present tends to be related to how close the research is to you: to your opinion, to your research, or to current knowledge (Swales and Feak, 2004). Some would argue that it gives the impression that your research is up-to-date and in the domain of current debates in your field. See Example 7.17.

Example 7.17 Reporting verb in the present

According to Findlen (1994) the world's first museums emerged in Italy in the 16th century. Analysing the context and processes of this emergence, she *writes:*

> Humanists, natural philosophers, and collectors were not just found **anywhere** in society. They inspected nature in a precisely demarcated setting, the museum, that took its place alongside the courts and academies of late Renaissance and Baroque Italy as a space in which learned and elite culture converged (Findlen 1994: 97, emphasis hers).

Source: Meyer, 2006: 17

Choice of tense in the clause or sentence where the information is reported

As well as the tense of the reporting verb, the tense in the clause where the cited information is reported is also significant. The choice depends on the meaning which you wish to convey. If the information reported refers to the results of a single study the past simple is used, as shown in Example 7.18.

Example 7.18 Reported findings in the past simple tense

Hamilton et al. (1980) found that asking participants to form an impression of a target person *led* to a greater degree of thematic organization of the presented information than did asking participants to memorise the information.

Source: Webb, 2003: 5

If the information reported reflects current knowledge or beliefs, or it is information which can be generalised, the present tense is more likely to be used (see Example 7.19).

Example 7.19 Reported findings in the present simple tense

Orbell and Sheeran (1998) suggest that there *are* four possible patterns of consistency between intentions and behaviour.

Source: Webb, 2003: 7

When checking the verb tenses of the citations in your writing, you could try reading your work aloud bearing in mind these guidelines or ask a friend to read it. If your writing sounds awkward, look again at the general principles for tense usage suggested above.

Effective and unacceptable citations

In this final section of the chapter, Example 7.20 offers a series of four extracts to illustrate acceptable and unacceptable uses of a source text. The aim is to demonstrate how plagiarism can occur.

Example 7.20 Acceptable and unacceptable uses of a source text

An extract from a sample source text is provided below; it is taken from *Communities of Practice: Learning, meaning and identity* by Étienne Wenger.

The source extract

Our institutions, to the extent that they address issues of learning explicitly, are largely based on the assumption that learning is an individual process, that it has a beginning and an end, that it is best separated from the rest of our activities, and that it is a result of teaching. Hence we arrange classrooms where students – free from the distractions of their participation in the outside world – can pay attention to a teacher or focus on exercises. We design computer-based training programs that walk students through individualized sessions covering reams of information and drill practice. To assess learning we use tests with which students struggle in one-to-one combat, where knowledge must be demonstrated out of context, and where collaborating is considered cheating. As a result, much of our institutionalized teaching and training is perceived by would-be learners as irrelevant, and most of us come out of this treatment feeling that learning is boring and arduous, and that we are not really cut out for it.

So, what if we adopted a different perspective, one that placed learners in the context of our lived experience of participation in the world? What if we assumed that learning is as much a part of our human nature as eating or sleeping, that it is both life-sustaining and inevitable, and that – given a chance – we are quite good at it? And what if, in addition, we assumed that learning is, in its essence, a fundamentally social phenomenon, reflecting our own deeply social nature as human beings capable of knowing? What kind of understanding would such a perspective yield on how learning takes place and on what is required to support it? In this book, I will try to develop such a perspective.

Source: Wenger, 1998: 3

Example 7.20a An acceptable direct quotation

When discussing conventional approaches to learning, Wenger (1998: 3) argues that education institutions

are largely based on the assumption that learning is an individual process, that it has beginning and an end, that it is best separated from the rest of our activities, and that it is a result of teaching.

Example 7.20b
An acceptable summary

Wenger (1998) speculates on how we might alter our approach to learning if we change our underpinning assumptions about the ways that individuals learn. In his view, learners tend to be alienated by the individualized approach to learning which still predominates in many institutions and he proposes that we should move towards a more social approach.

Example 7.20c An unacceptable
paraphrase/summary

Institutions make the incorrect assumption that learning is an individual process and it results from teaching. Students learn in classrooms where they focus on the teacher and exercises. Collaborating is regarded as cheating. Therefore, most students view learning as irrelevant, boring and arduous and don't believe that they are cut out for it (Wenger, 1998).

Although the source material is acknowledged in Example 7.20c and some of the wording has been changed or omitted, the structure and many of the phrases are the same as in the original text: 'that learning is an individual process'; '… institutionalised teaching and training is perceived by would-be learners as irrelevant … learning is boring and arduous, and that we are not really cut out for it'. In addition, the initial phrase in the citation, 'Institutions make the incorrect assumption that …' makes a stronger statement than Wenger in the original source, 'Our institutions … are largely based on the assumption …'. Thus it could be argued that the citation is misrepresenting the strength of the assertion being made by Wenger.

Example 7.20d
Unacceptable borrowing

Our institutions are largely based on the assumption that learning is an individual process. But what if we adopted a different viewpoint and assumed that learning is a fundamentally social phenomenon? How would this affect our understanding of learning and the way we facilitate it?

There is no acknowledgement of the cited author in Example 7.20d and the wording is very close to Wenger's original sentences despite the fact that much of the detail has been omitted.

Text matching software: Turnitin

When learning how to incorporate ideas from sources into your own writing, it can be difficult to know whether you are managing to paraphrase and summarise successfully or whether you may be falling into the trap of 'patchwork writing' (Hull and Rose 1989; Howard 1995) when your text is overly dependent on the phrases and wording of the cited authors. In order to find out how much of your writing is in your own words, it is possible to submit your work to an online text-matching service. Most universities subscribe to Turnitin (http://turnitin.com/static/products/index.php) or a similar software package. Through this service, you can submit your writing electronically and Turnitin compares it to all the writing stored on their databases, which include web sites, online journals, electronic books and electronically submitted student work. You then receive an originality report that identifies how much and which parts of your writing are identical to any of the electronic sources on the databases. The report is colour coded and, where there are matches, Turnitin identifies the source that the identical wording has come from. Each instance has to be looked at carefully but a match is likely to mean that it will be necessary to revise this part of the writing, either by paraphrasing and referencing correctly or, in some circumstances, it may be appropriate to add quotation marks and present the reference as a direct quote.

Although Turnitin may be used by tutors to check writing for plagiarism, in a more positive sense, it is a valuable tool for students enabling them to evaluate how well they are managing to paraphrase and summarise successfully. The highlighted parts of an originality report show where revisions can be made to avoid potential issues of plagiarism, before the writing is submitted to your supervisor. Turnitin also offers a service called WriteCheck, which can be used independently from a university to perform a text matching check.

It should, however, be noted that Turnitin does not check writing against printed books. Furthermore, originality reports must be read carefully as some parts of text that are highlighted may be valid matches and not an instance where revision is necessary, for example, short statements of common knowledge. Originality reports can be helpfully discussed between a student and tutor or amongst students in a tutorial to develop writing and understanding of referencing conventions.

Task 7.1 Analysing reference techniques in your own research field

Read the literature review in a thesis or dissertation in your field or read a section which includes a number of in-text references. Analyse the referencing techniques by working through the following activities and questions.

1. Identify all the citations.
2. Note whether they are integral or non-integral references.
3. Which are more common: integral or non-integral references?
4. Consider why the writer has chosen to use an integral or non-integral reference in each instance.
5. Ascertain whether each citation is a summary, generalisation or quotation.
6. Which type of citation – summary, generalisation or quotation – is most common?
7. Underline all the reporting verbs and note which ones are used.
8. Identify the verb tense of the reporting verbs.
9. Identify the verb tenses used in the clauses where cited information is presented.
10. Consider the possible reasons for all the tense choices.

Think about the features of citations that you have noted in this task and consider how it might influence your own acknowledgement of the work of others in your writing.

Summary

To summarise, this chapter has discussed:

- the reasons for in-text referencing;
- plagiarism and the various ways that it can occur;
- when a reference is required;
- the different referencing systems and their formats;
- integral and non-integral references and the possible reasons for using each style;
- summarising, paraphrasing, generalisations, and direct quotations;
- the range of reporting verbs and tense differences;
- disciplinary difference in relation to citation choices;
- the potential benefits of using online text-matching software.

8

Being critical

Chapter summary

It is not uncommon for supervisors to urge research students to be more critical when reviewing the literature for their research. However, it is not always straightforward to articulate what is meant by 'being critical'. This chapter offers some suggestions to help you adopt a more critical approach to both your reading and your writing, and gives examples from dissertations and theses which demonstrate how this has been achieved by researchers in a variety of disciplines.

In particular, we discuss:

- the difference between critical reading and critical writing;
- the different ways that we can show we are being critical in our writing;
- extracts from dissertations and theses and how they illustrate a variety of ways of being critical.

The difference between critical reading and critical writing

When discussing what it means to 'be critical', it is first of all important to distinguish between critical reading and critical writing. In Chapter 4, the meaning of critical reading was discussed and some prompt questions were suggested that can be used to ensure a critical approach when reading a text.

To recap briefly, in order to read critically you must:

1 Identify the author's arguments and the conclusions drawn in the text.
2 Evaluate the strength of the evidence that the author provides as support for his or her arguments and conclusions, asking a series of questions:

- is the evidence sufficient and relevant?
- are the authorities cited reliable?
- are the data and the interpretation of the data adequate to support the line of reasoning and the conclusions drawn in the text?
- if statistics are used as evidence, where do they come from and why have they been used? How are they relevant to the argument? Are the statistical tests appropriate and how have the statistics been interpreted?

3 Identify the implicit assumptions which underpin the text and decide on how these assumptions affect the arguments and conclusions that are presented, i.e. what political, moral and value judgements does an author seem to hold?

To write critically you should:

1 Present logical arguments which lead into your conclusions.
2 Provide sound evidence and reasons to support your argument.
3 In a dissertation or thesis literature review, you should evaluate, select, organize and categorize theories and findings to provide a coherent framework which forms the basis of your research.

As approaches to critical reading were considered in Chapter 4, the current focus is on critical writing.

Being critical in writing

When beginning to write about the literature in one's field, it may be tempting to include a summary and critique of every text that you have read. In other words, an attempt is made to embrace everything you have gleaned from your critical reading in your writing. However, effective critical writing is selective and you should include only the information that is relevant for your research. This is not to suggest that a detailed critique of each source text is unnecessary. Indeed, an essential step in the research process is critical reading of the related literature. An efficient researcher writes a summary and critique of each text they read, as suggested in Chapter 4, and then draws on the critiques when beginning to draft the literature review. As you plan and develop the steps of your argument (see Chapter 6), you selectively take the points from the related literature that provide support for your assertions.

The main strategies you can adopt in order to achieve a critical approach to the writing of your literature review are outlined below. These draw on characteristics which were originally proposed by Taylor (1989) and reformulated by Hart (1998). In the literature review, you are likely to use different strategies or combinations of these strategies at different points in your review. So, to give an overview, writing critically about the related literature to your research means:

- comparing and contrasting different theories, perspectives, concepts and terminology from the related literature and indicating the position you are taking for your own research;
- strategic and selective referencing to support the underpinning arguments which form the basis of your research;
- synthesising and reformulating arguments from two or more sources to create a new or more developed point of view;
- agreeing with, confirming or defending a finding or point of view through an analysis of its merits and limitations;
- conceding that an existing point of view has some strengths but qualifying your support of the position by highlighting certain weaknesses;
- rejecting a point of view and giving reasons for the rejection, e.g. inadequacy, lack of evidence, fallacies in the argument or research.

In connection with these techniques, there are some additional points which are important to remember when adopting a critical approach in your writing:

1 When referring to the work of others, it should be clear why you have selected certain work in your literature review and an adequate summary of their work or the aspect of their work that you are discussing should be provided. The type and length of the summary will depend on the purposes of the citation (see Chapter 4 for a discussion of different types of summary).
2 Being critical does not mean a complete demolition of someone else's work. In some fields, there is very little negative criticism of the work of others. You can show you are being critical, first, by the selection of what is relevant from the literature to provide a knowledge base and reasoned argument for your research and, second, by making connections between both the different sources you cite and between the cited work and your own research.
3 Negative critique of previous work is particularly likely to occur when showing how your own research fills a gap in the field, for example showing how a limitation in previous work creates a niche for your own. This could mean highlighting work that has not been done in the field; describing previous work which has flaws or limitations; or explaining how you want to look at something in another context or by using a different methodology to previous work. Negative critique might also occur when identifying the limitations of a theory or concept in accounting for a phenomenon that you are looking at in your research (see Example 8.4 below).

4 In a dissertation or thesis literature review, you join a critical debate in your field; it involves respectful critique and a certain amount of humility, acknowledging that you also might be challenged. It is important to focus your critique on the ideas, theories or findings and not the author; therefore choose your language carefully.

How different researchers adopt a critical approach in their writing

This section uses a series of examples and extracts to illustrate how a number of researchers approach 'being critical' when writing. The examples come from a range of disciplines and there is undoubtedly a significant amount of disciplinary difference in the way researchers adopt a critical approach in their writing. However, a detailed analysis of these differences is not the purpose of this chapter. There is a brief description before each example which explains how the writer is being critical and states the discipline in which the particular dissertation or thesis is situated.

In very general terms, in science, medicine and engineering fields 'being critical' tends to mean the selection of relevant previous work which illustrates the cumulative development of knowledge that has led into the current work. On the other hand, in the humanities and the social sciences, researchers are more likely openly to challenge and question the viewpoints of others in their writing and therefore more debate around different interpretations is evident. Machi and McEvoy (2009) suggest that it is useful to distinguish between two types of argument in a literature review: 1) the argument of discovery when you present what is known about a particular topic and 2) the argument of advocacy where you critique what is known to draw conclusions about relevant theories, concepts and findings that can then be used to underpin your own research. Both are important components of critical writing. Although, using this distinction, one might surmise that the argument of discovery is more likely to be more predominant in the science, medicine and engineering fields and the argument of advocacy in the humanities and social sciences, all literature reviews are almost certain to include both types of argument to differing extents. Often arguments of discovery and advocacy are interspersed and do not follow on from one another in a neat and predictable linear sequence. In some of the examples included below, I highlight how the writers have used each type of argument. It is helpful to be aware of these distinctions when constructing the arguments in your own literature review as it draws your attention to the difference between reporting what has been found out and the evaluation and interpretation of its significance for the research context and your own research study.

In Chapter 7, some of the features of disciplinary difference among in-text citation patterns were noted and these characteristics are indicative of the different disciplinary conventions which exist in relation to being critical. Task 8.1 at the end of the chapter encourages you to reflect specifically on the conventions in your own field.

Example 8.1

The first four extracts come from a doctoral thesis by Key-young Son from the field of East Asian studies. His work is based on research investigating strategies of engagement between North and South Korea from 1998 and 2003. The initial two extracts (Examples 8.1a and 8.1b) are from the introduction of the literature review chapter and they show how Key-young sets up his critical approach to the literature. The third and fourth extracts (Examples 8.1c and 8.1d) illustrate how he integrates the literature in a critical way.

In the early paragraph reproduced in Example 8.1a, Key-young is adopting a critical approach by explaining and beginning to justify the necessity to examine both Cold war and post-Cold war policies when discussing the policies of 'containment' and 'engagement'. I've italicised some phrases where he is using particularly evaluative language in relation his assertions, thus making his own stance clear to the reader. I refer to this example again in Chapter 9 when discussing the various ways to assert writer voice.

Example 8.1a An introduction
to the literature review chapter

eg → This chapter will analyse the two concepts of containment and engagement by dividing the post-WWII era into the Cold War and post-Cold War periods. While the main focus of this chapter is on the post-Cold War period when the debate on whether to contain or engage 'rogue states' has become *a particularly salient* policy issue, the contemporary debate on containment and engagement is *without doubt* closely linked to Cold War policies and initiatives, *making it fruitless to merely delve* into the post-Cold War situation. *In particular*, the Korean Peninsula, which in 1950–3 experienced the first 'hot war' of the Cold War period, is where both the structural and ideological legacies of the Cold War remain more or less intact.

Source: Son, 2004: 14–15

In the second extract Key-young shows how the comparison and contrast of three perspectives will be presented: realism, liberalism and constructivism. As explained above, being critical involves the analysis and comparison of different perspectives.

Example 8.1b An introduction to a section of the literature review

This section will first offer an historical overview of strategies of containment and engagement, followed by a review of Cold War-related theories from the three perspectives of realism, liberalism and constructivism.

Source: Son, 2004: 15

The italicised passages in the text in Example 8.1c show where Key-young introduces differences of opinion about the end of the Cold War. He starts off by outlining the standpoint of the realists. He does not negatively criticise the realists himself, but begins the critique by citing another source, Zubok, who disagrees with the realist interpretation. In this extract, Key-young is demonstrating a critical approach through his identification of the contrasting interpretations of a major event.

Example 8.1c Contrast of two different interpretations

eg → Realists attempt to explain the end of the Cold War from their observation that the overstretched Soviet Union could not maintain its status as a superpower in a fierce material competition with the United States (Wohlforth, 1994/5; Copeland, 1999/2000; Schweller and Wohlforth, 2000). *Nevertheless, Zubok (2001: 41) argued that it was wrong* to approach the collapse of the Soviet Union from the perspectives of 'economic crisis and external pressure', since the country had never been an economic superpower. *In line with this thought,*

> *constructivists are active in explaining* why the cold war was brought to an end in a peaceful way by using such ideational variables as cognitive learning, political entrepreneurship, identity politics, transnational networks and internalization of Western norms and values (Checkel, 1993 and 1997; Mendelson, 1993; Risse-Kappen, 1994; Lebow, 1994; Evangelista, 1995). *In particular*, these analysts attempt to identify what motivated the Soviet Union in the late 1980s to abandon confrontational modes of behaviour and retreat from eastern Europe voluntarily by highlighting the New Thinking of the Soviet leadership (Herman, 1996; Katzenstein, 1996a; Kowert and Legro, 1996; Checkel, 1998a).
>
> Source: Son, 2004: 32

Key-young points out on two occasions in Example 8.1d that 'realism' and 'liberalism' are inadequate theories to conceptualise the policy of engagement in the Korean Peninsula. He advocates the use of the constructivist approach. The italicised parts of the text show where he is pointing out and explaining the limitations of realism and liberalism, and where he is signalling the potential of constructivism. Using Machi and McEvoy's (2009) categorisation of arguments, this would be an example of the argument of advocacy.

Example 8.1d The limitations and potential of different theories

eg → If strategies of engagement pursue a behavioural change on the part of an enemy state, *realism and liberalism*, called 'problem-solving theories' (Cox, 1981: 128–9), *cannot address the problems properly because* they are based on the fixture of time and space, for example, the Cold War template or a clear enemy/friend concept, *thus tolerating no room* for any substantial change in policies or attitudes in the post-Cold War situation. *Hence, the appropriate use of a constructivist approach*, which is keen to identify clues to historical change, *is indispensable* in order to conceptualize comprehensive engagement. *At this juncture, a constructivist approach demonstrates the potential* to offer an analytical account of the process of rapprochement between adversaries by identifying signs of structural and domestic change and guiding policies in the right direction during the murky moments of change, *while realism and liberalism are apt to solve problems in a rather static international environment.*

Source: Son, 2004: 54

Example 8.2

The next three extracts (Examples 8.2a, 8.2b, and 8.2c) are from a doctoral thesis in psychology produced by Thomas Webb which has already been cited in previous chapters. Tom's work is based on experimental research investigating how people self-regulate their behaviour in order to achieve their goals.

Example 8.2a shows how the current research has a different focus to previous work. Tom clearly recognises previous work and acknowledges the important findings (arguments of discovery). He also identifies on three separate occasions that there are omissions and limitations in previous work. He then uses these weaknesses to lead into and provide justification for his three aims at the end of the chapter (arguments of advocacy).

Example 8.2a The scope of previous research and the niche for the current study

eg → There is little controversy about the importance of goals in the study of human action. Indeed, Locke (1969) argued that goal-directedness is a cardinal attribute of the behaviour of living organisms – goals are the starting point of the wilful control of action (Gollwitzer and Moskowitz, 1996). However, the majority of research into goals has been concerned with goal setting and goal content rather than with goal striving (Gollwitzer and Moskowitz, 1996). For example, we have a great deal of research that contrasts different goals on a dimension of interest (e.g., specific vs. vague goals, proximal vs. distal goals, Locke and Latham, 1990), but far less information about what happens once a person has decided to pursue a goal. The usual answer is that people's level of motivation (need or drive to attain the goal) will determine their success (e.g., Ajzen, 1991; Rogers, 1983). However, to date, there has been no systematic review of the causal relation between motivation and behaviour. Moreover, available correlational evidence suggests that motivation is not sufficient to ensure goal attainment. Research suggests that volitional processes such as implementation intentions may be required to ensure that motivation is translated into action. However, previous research has assumed – but not tested – the discriminant validity of motivation and volition, and has failed to address the question of why such strategies may prove effective. The aim of the present thesis is to examine the causal role of goal intentions on behaviour, to determine the joint impact of goal intentions and implementation intentions on behaviour, and to investigate the mechanism by which implementation intentions influence behaviour.

Source: Webb, 2003: 1–2

In Example 8.2b, a more specific critique of a particular group of studies is illustrated. In the first paragraph, Tom summarises the findings from correlational studies with regard to the relationship between intentions and behaviour (argument of discovery). He then goes on to identify three weaknesses with correlational studies and proposes an alternative which he is going to examine in the following chapter (argument of advocacy).

Example 8.2b Weaknesses of a particular type of study

eg → Correlational studies show that intentions are reliably associated with behaviour. A meta-analysis of 10 meta-analyses by Sheeran (2002) found that, based on 422 studies and a sample size of 82,107, intentions accounted for 28% of the variance in behaviour ($r_+ = .53$). In the context of the Theory of Planned Behaviour (TPB), Armitage and Connor's (2001) meta-analysis of 185 studies found that intentions accounted for 22% of the variance in behaviour ($r_+ = .47$). Calculation of fail-safe N indicated that 26,235 studies showing that intentions are not predictive of behaviour would be required in order to be able to conclude that intention has no significant relationship with behaviour (for similar findings, see meta-analyses by Ajzen, 1991; Godin and Kok, 1996; Hausenblas, Carron, and Mack, 1997; van den Putte, 1991).

However, a number of problems are encountered when attempting to infer causation from correlational studies. First, many studies employ cross-sectional designs which means that reports of intentions and behaviour may be subject to consistency or self-presentational biases that artificially inflate the relationship between intention and behaviour (cf. Budd, 1987).

Second, correlational studies do not rule out the possibility that past behaviour caused intention. In other words, intentions may simply reflect how the person has behaved in the past rather than a behavioural decision. For example, if you usually exercise twice a week, when asked about your exercise intentions for next week, you may not actively engage in a decision making process. Instead your intention to exercise next week may be based on your previous exercise behaviour.

Third, although longitudinal designs that correlate intentions at time 1 with behaviour at time 2 preclude a path from past behaviour to intention, problems still

(Continued)

(Continued)

arise when inferring causation. For example, longitudinal designs may be subject to the third variable problem whereby a third – unmeasured – variable influences both intention and behaviour and creates a spurious correlation between the two. Indeed, Wegner and Wheatley (1999) suggested that 'we can never be sure that our thoughts cause our actions, as there could always be unconscious causes that have produced them both' (p. 482).

To my mind, the best way to determine if a person's intention causes their subsequent behaviour is to manipulate intention and observe whether there is a corresponding change in behaviour. Chapter 2 presents a quantitative review of 30 such studies in an attempt to quantify the causal impact of intention on behaviour.

Source: Webb, 2003: 3–4

In Example 8.2c we can see how Tom references strategically and selects relevant points from the literature to support the assertions which he makes in the first sentence of each paragraph. The signalling words which make connections between the citations are, again, italicised

Example 8.2c Showing connections between different source texts

eg → One reason why inclined abstainers fail to act on their intentions might be that they simply forget them. *In a study of* breast self-examination (BSE) by Orbell, Hodgkins, and Sheeran (1997), 70% of participants who intended to perform BSE in the next month and failed to do so endorsed forgetting as the reason for their non-performance. *Similarly,* in a study of exercise behaviour by Milne, Orbell, and Sheeran (2002), 17% of inclined abstainers reported forgetting as their reason for failing to exercise (other reasons included 'being too busy' and 'not getting around to it').

Related to forgetting is the issue of competing action tendencies (Kuhl, 1984). *For instance,* achievement of one's goal to run a marathon requires that one balances training with competing social commitments. Shah and Kruglanski (2002) *operationalised these ideas* by repeatedly priming participants with an unrelated, secondary goal while they tried to pursue the primary or focal goal.

Source: Webb, 2003: 8

The extract in Example 8.3a shows how Morgan first provides a contemporary context for the research described in the thesis by discussing the museum as a contact zone and, second, identifies the significant features of a contact zone for the current research. One important aspect of being critical is showing the

Example 8.3

Examples 8.3a and 8.3b are extracts from a thesis in the field of sociology written by Morgan Meyer. The focus of the research is on the ways that scientific knowledge is produced in museums.

way that your own work connects with the literature. Once again we can identify the argument of discovery in the first part of the extract when current beliefs about museums are presented and the argument of advocacy after the direct quotation when Morgan draws out what is relevant for the current work.

Example 8.3a Connections between the literature and the current study

eg → Apart from bringing together different people, museums are also contact zones in the sense that objects geographically and historically separated are drawn together. In a natural history museum, for example, species from different parts of the world and from different periods in time are brought together. But not only does the museum classify, preserve and manage such diverse objects, some of these objects inhabit multiple worlds at the same time:

The intersectional nature of the museum's shared work creates objects which inhabit multiple worlds simultaneously, and which must meet the demands of each one […] In natural history work, boundary objects are produced when sponsors, theorists and amateurs collaborate to produce representations of nature. Among these objects are specimens, field notes, museums and maps of particular territories (Star and Griesemer 1989: 408).

For the present work, two elements of the above quote are central: the museum's intersectional nature and its involvement in the production of boundary objects (these will be discussed in section four). In this view, the museum does two things: it is a contact zone, a place where some walls are made and unmade, and it is an institution that produces things (objects but also knowledge).

Source: Meyer, 2006: 19

In Example 8.3b Morgan attributes different pieces of information to different sources as part of the construction of his argument which emphasises the research focus on a 'museum without walls'. In the latter part of the example, a series of related assertions are each attributed to an individual source.

Example 8.3b The strategic synthesis of sources to support the author's overall argument

eg → Apart from the museum's intersectional nature and its involvement in the production of things and knowledge, I will take on board a third element. I am interested in the Museum as a 'museum without walls'. It has been argued that the 'museum without walls' was the third step in the spatial evolution of museums (see Hetherington, 1996: 153). First, there was a 'pre-museum' space: collections were localised in palaces, private homes, churches, gardens, etc. Then, the classical museum developed during the 17th and 18th centuries to become a 'museum with walls'. Finally, the 'museum without walls' developed. Whereas for Malraux (1965) the museum without walls is located in books, brought about through the reproduction of art, 'unwalling' happens through other means, in other places too. Hetherington lists three factors involved in the breakdown of the walls of the museum: forces of commercialisation, the emergence of the heritage industry, and popular interests in sites of historical interest outside the confines of the museum (see Hetherington 1996: 154). We can add five more elements. First, democratic values and, especially for natural history museums, environmental and social movements have drawn places and people formerly outside of the museum project into the heart of its preoccupation. Second, while museums still predominantly display 'things' (Macdonald, 2004) some museums have shifted their allegiance from real objects to real experiences (Hein, 2000: 87) and can break down their walls more easily. Also, third, in the 'information age' with its digital information networks and databases, the museum's collection and expert information becomes linked to other organizations, and identities become blurred (Keene, 1998: 17). Fourth, in theoretical terms too, the 'museum refuses to stand still' (Hudson, 1998) as the concept of what a museum is has enlarged over the years (Hooper-Greenhill, 2000b: 180) and as the museum's walls opened up to the increasing interest of anthropologists, philosophers, economists, etc. alongside more classical academic work in history or in the arts. Finally, it has been argued that the walls between science and art are crumbling in the museum (Van Praet, 1995; see also Macdonald, 2003).

Source: Meyer, 2006: 20–1

Example 8.4 Describing a theory, acknowledging its usefulness and pointing out its limitations

The extract below is from Étienne Wenger's PhD dissertation which was based on an ethnographic study of sociocultural communities. In this short extract, he summarises key aspects of Bourdieu's concept of 'habitus', and briefly acknowledges its usefulness before pointing out his view of its weaknesses. The author's explanation of habitus is interspersed with his critique of the concept and it is contrasted throughout to a central feature of his own research, 'communities of practice'. He uses the limitations of the concept of habitus as justification for proposing the notion of community of practice.

The italicised parts of the text highlight examples of language which signal positive acknowledgement of Bourdieu's concept of habitus, indicate limitations of the concept, and signal contrast with the concept of communities of practice.

eg → Pierre Bourdieu (1977, 1980) has developed the ... concept of the habitus, a set of cultural principles *that generate in a coherent fashion* the modes of activities, the life style and tastes, and the interests of a group, usually a social class. It is for him the determinant factor in the way people shape their sense-making. *I find the habitus to be a very useful* concept. But the habitus *differs from* the notion of community of practice in being one of these broad structural principles, an emerging property of the social world. As such, *it tends to overlook* the social forms that we construct locally as we engage in practice and in reflection on practice. It *overlooks* the day-to-day mechanisms of co-participation in practice, of construction of the self in perceptible communities that give it local coherence through shared practice; these give rise through practical co-engagement to what can be observed as a habitus. This broadly structural nature of the habitus *makes it difficult to account* for its reproduction and evolution time. For Bourdieu, this seems to be mostly located in the family, which becomes a privileged unit of reproduction through a dichotomy between public and private life: the habitus is acquired in early childhood and becomes an inescapable, closed lifeworld. In short, the habitus has a social realm, but *it does not have* a social body. This is where the *concretely inhabited character* of communities of practice *provides an important mediating level of analysis* in structuring co-participation in practice both within communities of practice and in the articulation among them.

Source: Wenger, 1990: 150–1

Example 8.5 Making connections between cited authors and with the current research

The following extract is from a PhD thesis in the field of information studies written by Ruth Bacigalupo. In the first and second paragraphs below, Ruth groups authors together who support the notion of a process view of information management in organisations and she also attributes specific examples of this point of view to particular authors. Then, from

(Continued)

(Continued)

the second half of the second paragraph to the end of the extract, she makes connections with her own research topic by clarifying how she is using the term 'information management'. The phrases which signal connections with the current research have been italicised

eg → A process view of information management in organisations has been adopted by some authors (for example, Davenport 1993; Best 1996; Choo 1998; Orna 1999). Davenport (1997) uses the term 'information technology' to describe the holistic management of information in an organisation. The approach is user centred rather than focused on technology. An organisation's entire information environment is emphasised; this includes culture, processes and behaviour, politics, and technology. 'Information ecologists' put how people produce, share, understand and use information at the centre of their work (Davenport 1997: 5). Choo (1998) views information management broadly to include management of information processes, information resources and information technologies. Organisations are not viewed as static but as dynamic and open in character; they can be viewed as 'societies of minds'. The basic goal of information management is to 'harness information resources and information capabilities so that the organisation learns and adapts to its changing environment' (Choo 1998: 24).

Broad definitions of 'information management' and 'information' are necessary in any environment; that is, holistic definitions that are not IT led (Davenport 1997; Best 1996; Parsons 1996; Wilson 1985). However, the term 'information management' should be treated with caution because it can be used on a number of levels and in different contexts in different organisations (Feenev 1996). *As far as the literature and indeed this study is concerned* 'information management' is a term used both to describe an approach (philosophy and theory behind information management practice), and also on a more specific level to describe the behaviour of health visitors in relation to their information use/handling.

Information management research for the purpose of this study is defined as: a holistic research approach to the way health visitors use information resources, both internal and external, to aid their community development work. 'Information' refers to the information resources (products and processes) health visitors use to help them carry out community development work (as a facet of public health activities). Looking at the use of information resources in this way may also highlight barriers to handling information, for example information overload.

Source: Bacigalupo, 2000: 15–16

Example 8.6 Comparing and contrasting models from different authors

The following example is from Dino Ovcina's MSc dissertation in the field of International Business and Management. He has conducted a case study researching a US retail company's entry into a Latin American market. In the extract from his literature review below, he presents different models for entering new markets. He adopts a critical approach by comparing and contrasting the models, highlighting their limitations and moving from the more general models to those that more specifically relate to the focus of his research: emerging markets and the retail industry. Phrases which show connections between authors and limitations are italicised.

2.3 Choosing the Right Market (Where)

Choosing in what country or group of countries to invest/enter and which entry mode to choose is another challenging process facing companies. According to Hollensen (2004) factors affecting this decision are:

Internal factors;

External factors;

Desired mode characteristics;

Transaction specific behavior.

Similar factors are shown in Peng's (2006) comprehensive model of foreign entries. *However, the main focus in this model* is on the internal factors in terms of resource based considerations on firm specific assets and external factors in terms of Industry-based considerations on the degree of competiveness and institution based considerations on country risk. *Both Peng (2006) and Hollensen (2004)* are speaking about entering markets in general; *hence their models need to be combined with scholars* who have investigated the topic when it comes to emerging markets and retailing industry. *In particular, external factors, when entering emerging markets, are considered by scholars as being of key importance.* Cavusgil et al. (2002) mentions among others factors the history of country risk, the GDP growth rate, and the attraction of gaining a competitive advantage from a developed country company perspective. Alexander and Doherty (2009) have studied the issue from a retailer perspective. They suggest dividing the evaluation process into two stages: market scanning and market research. Market scanning is mainly based on secondary data and should give a quick picture of pros and cons of several potential markets. Market research on the other hands is a more complex and in depth process that requires a large amount of resources. This stage is mainly based on primary research, which

(Continued)

155

(Continued)

means that only a limited number of markets can be investigated. *Furthermore,* Alexander and Doherty (2009: 235) give an overview of assessment criteria that can be used for this evaluation. *These criteria are similar to criteria given by Dawson et al. (2006)* which include (1) geographic distance, (2) cultural proximity, (3) maturity of the distribution system, and (4) economical and political stability.

Source: Ovcina, 2010: 17–18

Task 8.1 Critical writing in your own research field

In a sample dissertation or thesis from your field, look at a section from a literature review and answer the following questions.

1 In the light of the explanations and examples in this chapter, identify ways in which the writer of the dissertation or thesis is being critical.
2 Are there any examples of negative criticism by the writer of the cited work? If so, analyse the context in which the negative comment occurs. For example, does the writer use the negative comment as a way of making a space to justify his/her own research?
3 In your field, is it common practice to be negative about the work of others or is it more common to positively and selectively acknowledge the ideas that underpin your research? If you are not sure, discuss this question with your supervisor.

Consider your own writing. In what ways are you being critical? Could you adopt any of the strategies advocated in this chapter to achieve a more critical approach in your writing?

Summary

To summarise, this chapter has considered:

- the difference between critical reading and critical writing;
- the ways in which one can adopt a critical approach in one's writing;
- a number of extracts from theses and dissertations which give examples of the different ways being critical.

9

Foregrounding writer voice

Chapter summary

In the previous chapter, we discussed the range of ways in which you can adopt a critical approach in your writing. In Chapter 7, we looked at the variety of in-text citation patterns that can be used when referring to the work of others. In this chapter we will further develop the ideas explored in the preceding two chapters and in particular consider how you can demonstrate that you are being critical by foregrounding writer voice in your dissertation or thesis. The chapter will discuss the meaning of writer voice, moving on to the range of ways to assert your own voice in your writing, i.e. by maximising the potential of:

- text organisation;
- the use of personal pronouns;
- the choice of citation pattern;
- the evaluative nature of reporting verbs;
- the use of evaluative adjectives, adverbs and phrases.

What is writer voice?

The foregrounding of writer voice refers to the way that you assert your own presence in your dissertation or thesis in relation to the content and to your readers; in other words, how you create your authorial self (Ivanič, 1998). When writing your literature review, there are two main ways of presenting your own voice assertively. The first is by taking control of the text and leading your reader through the content. This can be done by making your own assertions with appropriate citations to provide support, and by including explicit linking words and phrases to show connections between citations and the different sections and chapters in the text. The second is by making your own position clear in relation to the source material that you incorporate and being explicit about how you will be drawing on particular aspects of previous work for your own research.

When writer voice is brought to the fore, it is clear that you are using your source texts to suit your own purposes rather than hiding behind the authority of the cited authors. This chapter aims to give some suggestions about how you can organise your text and use language and citation patterns strategically to assert your own voice successfully in your writing. However, before offering some guidance and illustrating effective practice, Example 9.1 shows how the writer's voice can remain in the background due both to overdependence on source material and to the way that the source material is introduced.

Example 9.1 Writer voice in the background

eg → Swales (1990: 58) defines genre as 'a class of communicative events, the members of which share some set of communicative purposes'. Berkenkotter and Huckin (1995) list some of the generic forms through which academics communicate, such as lab reports, conference papers and journal articles. They emphasize the importance of being familiar with these genres to progress professionally. Johns (1997: 21) explains how we build up our genre knowledge by 'repeated contextualised experiences with texts'. For Miller (1984) genres are a means of performing social actions. She explains that genres develop as a result of our typified actions which occur in recurring and similar situations.

While this extract includes viewpoints of different authors on the topic of 'genre', the writer does not make any explicit statements about how each author either builds on or challenges the opinions of others. In other words, no connections between the references are specifically highlighted by the writer. Each sentence begins with the name of a cited author or a pronoun referring to a cited author. This results in the text being dominated by the source authors instead of emphasising the writer's purposes for including a discussion about genre. Every sentence in the extract is attributable to a cited author and the writer's position is not made clear in relation to the topic.

The organisation of the text

The strategies described in Chapter 8 for adopting a critical approach to your writing introduced techniques for organising your text effectively. These strategies will be revisited in this section with a more explicit focus on the ways that writer voice is brought to the fore. In addition to including new examples from sample dissertations and theses, I refer back to some of the extracts in Chapter 8 to indicate how they illustrate salient points about writer voice.

Unattributed assertions followed by support from citations

A very effective way of foregrounding your own voice is to make an unattributed assertion, that is a statement which is not referenced to another source, and then follow it up with viewpoints, findings or information from source texts to support or elaborate on this assertion.

In Example 9.2 from Key-young's thesis, the first sentence is a statement by the writer about 'containment' which is not referenced to another source. This is therefore an example of writer voice being brought to the fore. The unattributed assertion is then balanced by a citation which elaborates on the meaning of 'containment'. By presenting the citation after an unattributed statement, Key-young is using the reference for his own purposes and is not allowing the cited author to dominate.

Example 9.2 An initial unattributed assertion

eg → Containment is a by-product of the Cold War in which the United States and other Western states made all-out efforts to contain the ever-multiplying sphere of 'red' stretching across the Eurasian continent. In his seminal book, *Strategies of Containment*, Gaddis (1982) sought to analyze containment in terms of 'strategies' as a way to elucidate this illusive concept, which had undergone mutations and transformations through successive US administrations.

Source: Son, 2004: 15

See Example 8.3a for another example of this strategy.

Making explicit connections between citations

When presenting your citations, you can assert your voice by showing explicitly how they relate to each other. By highlighting the connections, you bring your own voice to the fore by controlling how source texts are presented in relation to one another. The following examples illustrate ways to signal difference and similarity respectively between citations:

- However, Gill (2006) takes a different approach …
- In the same way, Porter (2005) uses the term holistically …

In Example 9.3 Key-young uses the word 'while' to indicate contrasting viewpoints on the meaning of détente between the two cited authors, Halliday and Gaddis.

Example 9.3 Showing contrast between references

eg → Halliday (1986: 205–6) viewed the Nixon-Kissinger strategy of détente as an attempt to preserve US hegemony with a comprehensive package of punishments and inducements, while Gaddis (1982: 314) stressed that the initiative, based on Kennan's strategy of containment, was aimed at integrating the Soviet economy with that of the Western world to such an extent that the Soviet Union would have no motive for shattering the status quo.

Source: Son, 2004: 20

Look back at Examples 8.1c and 8.2c for further illustrations of this strategy.

Summary and evaluation of source material

Another technique which was illustrated in the previous chapter involves summarising the relevant point that you are citing from a source text and then making an evaluative comment about this material.

In the extract in Example 9.4, taken from the field of sociolinguistics, Ei leen Lee first of all summarises Fishman's Graded Intergenerational Disruption Scale and then gives her evaluative comments using words such as 'successful' and 'realistic' to indicate her view of the scale. She introduces a qualifying comment about the applicability of the scale with the signal 'However' (italics have been used to highlight these features).

Example 9.4 Summary, evaluation and application of source material

eg → The term [Reversing language shift (RLS)] covers both the diagnosis and assessment of the status of an endangered language as well as the ameliorative priorities that should be taken to alleviate the threat of extinction a language may face in the process of language shift (LS). The basis of RLS theory proposed by Fishman (1991) is manifested in the Graded Intergenerational Disruption Scale (GIDS) framework ... [which includes] an eight-stage description of ... the varying degrees of language endangerment.

Stage 8: Social isolation of few remaining speakers of minority language

Stage 7: Minority language used by older but not younger generation

Stage 6: Minority language is passed on from generation to generation and used in the community

Stage 5: Literacy in the minority language

Stage 4: Formal, compulsory education available in the minority language

Stage 3: Use of the minority language in less specialized work areas involving interaction with majority language speakers

Stage 2: Lower government services and mass media available in the minority language

Stage 1: Some use of minority language available in the central government and national media. (Based on Fishman, 1991; 2001)

...

So far, as a heuristic tool the Scale has been *successful* in providing information on how to assess the language endangerment status of a language. ... *However*, since all sociolinguistic situations vary, *it is necessary to adapt* the GIDS model to local conditions ... . In its essence, the GIDS provides a *realistic* diagnosis of the LS situation of the language under threat and a systematic approach to correct the imbalance.

Source: Adapted from: Lee, 2003: 82–3, 98

Examples 8.2b and 8.4 also demonstrate this strategy of a summary followed by evaluative comment.

Overall summary at end of section or chapter

A further way to incorporate writer voice into the text is to write a summary at the end of a section or chapter in which you recap or reiterate the main points of relevance from the sources cited in the section. This is usually signalled by words, such as 'thus' or 'to summarise'.

The summary in Example 9.5 appears at the end of a section in a thesis from the field of psychology about 'implementation intentions' in relation to 'behaviour'. Tom summarises and offers an interpretation of the citations that have appeared previously.

He then goes on to signal a gap in previous research and thus a niche for his own study. In this summary paragraph, the writer's voice is clearly dominant. The non-integral reference to Gollwitzer serves to support the concluding statement made by the writer which is introduced by the phrase 'In sum'. The phrase 'Two processes appear to be responsible for' explicitly signals the conclusions that Tom is drawing from the citations that have been discussed in the section (italics have been used to emphasise these 'signals').

Example 9.5 End of section summary

eg → *In sum,* by forming implementation intentions, people can strategically switch from conscious and effortful action initiation (guided by goal intentions) to having their goal-directed actions effortlessly elicited by the specified situational cues (Gollwitzer et al., in press). *Two processes appear to be responsible for* the success of implementation intentions: heightened accessibility of the situational cue and a strengthened association between the cue and the behaviour. *However, research to date has been concerned primarily with* the consequences of associative strength (i.e., the features of automaticity described above) and *has failed to directly examine whether* the strength of association between situation and action mediates the impact of implementation intentions on behaviour. Chapter 5 describes this important test.

Source: Webb, 2003: 16

The use of personal pronouns

The most explicit way to foreground writer voice is to use the personal pronouns 'I' or 'we'. This technique offers a powerful means of asserting your own presence and identity in your writing. However, due to the variety of viewpoints and conventions regarding the use of personal pronouns in academic writing, it is an issue worth discussing with your supervisor early on in your dissertation or thesis writing process as it can have a major effect on the way that you present yourself in your writing.

There are a number of different purposes for which personal pronouns can be used (Hyland, 1999; Ivanič, 1998; Tang and John, 1999):

- to explain activities undertaken by the researcher;
- to explain how the text is structured;
- to explain the researcher's findings or results;
- to describe personal experiences or reflections;
- to present a claim or point of view.

In relation to the literature review, the second and final functions of the use of personal pronouns are the most relevant.

Some research students may initially feel reluctant to adopt the use of personal pronouns as there remains a common perception that personal pronouns are 'not allowed' in academic writing. However in many social sciences and humanities fields, the inclusion of personal pronouns has become widespread and may even be expected in a number of contexts.

It is true that in some other disciplines, for example, in science, engineering and medicine, where knowledge creation is assumed to be more impersonal and objective, it is a good idea to be cautious about adopting this practice. Generally speaking, in these fields, the process and results of a research study are given more prominence than the researchers who conduct the research and obtain the results.

Research by Hyland (1999, 2004) has found there is disciplinary difference in the use of personal pronouns among published authors, not only in connection with the actual personal pronoun selected but also in relation to the purposes for which they are adopted and the verbs which appear with the pronouns. In his corpus of peer-reviewed research articles, Hyland found there was a far greater use of personal pronouns in the humanities and social sciences, in particular singular personal pronouns. The research revealed that singular personal pronouns (I, me, my) are rare in science and engineering fields whereas plural personal pronouns (we, us, our) are more common. In those fields personal pronouns were more likely to be used to describe research activities, procedures, or the structure of the text; verbs such as *measure, analyse, note* or *discuss* are common. In contrast, in the social sciences and humanities, researchers used personal pronouns to indicate their stance or opinion on an idea or to make a claim; verbs such as *argue, think,* and *propose* are more widespread.

As Hyland's research suggests, the use of 'we' is often perceived to be more acceptable than 'I', particularly in the disciplines of science, engineering and medicine. 'We' may be used because research has been conducted collaboratively although this is less likely to be the case when writing up your research for a masters or doctoral degree as your dissertation or thesis is generally an individual piece of work for the purposes of assessment.

'We' may also be used to establish a rapport with the readers and to give a sense of the writer and reader exploring ideas together. For example, at the beginning of this chapter, my initial sentences demonstrate this:

> In the previous chapter, we discussed the range of ways in which you can adopt a critical approach in your writing. In Chapter 7, we looked at the variety of in-text citation patterns that can be used when referring to the work of others. In this chapter we will further develop the ideas explored in the preceding two chapters …

Another function of 'we' is to represent people in general, for example, 'We know that the use of mobile phone texting and the Internet is changing the way language is used'. In this final sense, the use of 'we' is not really a means to foreground writer voice although it does serve to enhance a sense of community between the writer and readers.

In the subsections which follow, some examples demonstrate two important functions of personal pronouns: to take explicit responsibility for a viewpoint and to show the literature review structure.

Using personal pronouns to take explicit responsibility for a point of view

In Example 9.6 taken from Ei leen's thesis in the field of sociolinguistics, the author uses personal pronouns on three occasions to assert her own point of view in relation to the chosen methodology for her research. On one of these occasions she uses 'we' to draw the readers along with her in her search for a suitable methodology.

In addition to her use of personal pronouns, she projects her own voice into the text by the presentation of an argument in the first paragraph which is unattributed. Within this paragraph, the adjective 'insufficient' is strongly evaluative of an ethnographic approach. She consolidates her argument in the second paragraph by referring to two authors' definitions of 'critical ethnography', highlighting the connections between the two authors with the phrase 'Both these definitions imply…' and then introduces her own interpretation of the term with the phrase 'In my view …'.

**Example 9.6 The use of 'I' to
present a point of view**

 eg → Towards Critical Ethnography

No matter how distinctive a research methodology may be for a type of research there are areas in the methodology that need to be adapted and refined to suit the particular scope of a study. Research questions dictate the choice of research tools; similarly, the scope of a study helps define the specific types of relationship, processes and direction the research methodology will take. Taking into consideration the scope of the intended study, it is *insufficient* to just adopt an ethnographic approach and aim at an emic and etic account of what seems to be taking place in the community and the multicultural setting. To be specific, *I am in favour* of a more interactive methodology that (i) draws from both the researcher and the researched (ii) brings the researcher and the researched closer to each other's perspective and in doing so, directs both parties to act independently for their individual goals.

To achieve the above, *we need a paradigm shift* in the methodology, from conventional to critical ethnography which *according to Nwenmely (1996: 47)* is a 'more socially responsive ethnography that has the potential of effecting change.' *Thomas (1993: 4) defines* critical ethnography as 'conventional ethnography with a political purpose.' *Both these definitions imply* active roles for the researcher as well as for the subjects. *In my view,* critical ethnography is a variant of conventional ethnography; it retains some of the features of conventional ethnography while the expectation of the researcher as well as the participants to take active roles in the research adds a new dimension to conventional ethnographic research. This methodology encourages a two-way (interactive), reflective and collaborative research process which empowers both the researcher and the researched.

Source: Lee, 2003: 119–20

Using personal pronouns to
show the structure of the literature review

Examples 9.7 and 9.8 are from a sociological studies doctoral thesis which has been cited in previous chapters. Example 9.7, taken from the Introduction, shows how Morgan uses the personal pronoun to give an overview of how he is going to organise his writing.

Example 9.7 The use of 'I' to show text organisation

eg → The thesis is divided into eight chapters. In Chapter One, I bring together different theoretical approaches. First, I am concerned with the spaces in which science takes place: the laboratory, the field, and the museum. Then, science studies and in particular actor-network theory will be discussed. Thereafter, I will consider the boundaries of science. I will discuss concepts such as 'boundary work' and 'boundary objects' before focusing on one particular boundary, that between amateurs and professionals.

Source: Meyer, 2006: 8

In Example 9.8, which is the first paragraph of Morgan's literature review, we also see how he is using 'I' to make claims and express his opinion: 'I suggest' and 'I argue'. He is introducing the argument which will be further developed in the chapter as a whole.

Example 9.8 The use of 'I' to introduce a central argument

Chapter 1: Exploring the boundaries of science in a museum of natural history

eg → A literature review does not simply review a body of literature. It has to do more than this: it has to identify and propose how to fill a gap. The absence I help to create and attempt to fill is the following one. I suggest that academic work has insufficiently looked into museums as sites of knowledge production and that the relation between amateurs and professionals is under-researched. In science studies in particular the relations between scientists and non-scientists, expert and lay, have received little attention until recently (Callon and Rabeharisoa 2003). I argue that museums of natural history deserve more scrutiny and that actor-network theory is a useful – if limited – approach for this endeavour.

Source: Meyer, 2006: 12

The choice of citation pattern

As the previous sections show, a significant challenge when incorporating references into your writing is to achieve a successful balance between the sources of information that you cite and your own voice. If you are over dependent on sources, you may run the risk of being challenged on the grounds of lack of original thought. On the other hand, if you do not include enough references, you may be criticised for making too many unsubstantiated claims. Generally speaking you can achieve the appropriate balance through the use of unattributed statements followed by a variety of citation patterns, each of which matches your purpose for including a reference.

Table 9.1 provides a helpful summary of how the relationship between the voice of the cited author and the writer varies according to citation pattern, bearing in mind that it is the overall context in which the citations are used that ultimately determines the balance achieved. The term 'writer' refers to the writer of the dissertation or thesis and the 'author' to the cited source' in this context.

TABLE 9.1   Propositional responsibility and textual voice

Propositional responsibility	Textual voice		Example
	Writer	Author	
Writer	Central	Absent	Global warming is a serious risk to the planet.
Shared	Dominant	Subordinate	Global warming is a serious risk to the planet (Clark 2006).
Shared	Corresponding		As Clark (2006) points out, global warming is a serious risk to the planet.
Shared	Subordinate	Dominant	Clark (2006) points out that global warming is a serious risk to the planet.
Author	Delayed	Central	Clark (2006) argues that global warming ... According to Clark (2006), global warming ...

Source: Adapted from Groom, 2000: 22

In the right-hand column, there are examples of the principal citation patterns from which you can choose when referring to the work of others. The other columns provide an analysis for each pattern describing whether the cited author or the writer of the dissertation is responsible for the content in the text and, hence, whether author or writer voice dominates.

The first column, 'propositional responsibility', indicates whether the writer or author is responsible for the content of the information being presented. Thus, in the first example, where there is no reference included, the writer is responsible for the assertion and there is no author voice present. The central two columns provide further information about whose voice dominates. For instance, if stating 'Clark points out ...', it suggests that the writer is accepting the author's claim whereas if you use 'Clark argues that ...', the writer is implying that he or she will at a later point make his or her viewpoint clear or that he or she will present an alternative viewpoint from another author.

As Table 9.1 suggests, you can bring writer voice to the fore most successfully by using non-integral references. Indeed, in Chapter 7, we discussed how non-integral references are the most common citation pattern among published authors in the majority of disciplines as they enable writers to control the text more successfully. However, in the humanities and social sciences disciplines in particular, the inclusion of integral references is helpful when presenting different viewpoints and for demonstrating both the level of commitment that the dissertation writer has to the cited work, and that a cited author has towards his or her own work (see the following section on the evaluative potential of reporting verbs).

In the Example 9.9, writer voice is brought to the fore through use of non-integral citation patterns.

Example 9.9 Foregrounding writer voice with non-integral references

eg → President Richard Nixon's credentials as a staunch anti-communist political figure helped him to thwart criticism from the right when he sought to build better relations with the Soviet Union and China (Garthoff 1985). In short, détente could be defined as 'a mixed competitive–collaborative relationship between global superpowers' with contrasting ideologies and different worldviews (Breslauer 1983: 336).

Source: Son, 2004: 20

Examples 7.8 and 8.3b also show how the writer successfully manages the text through the use of non-integral references.

The evaluative potential of different reporting verbs

In Chapter 7, I introduced the different categories of reporting verb according to whether they represent doing, thinking or discussion activities. We also considered which reporting verbs have been found to be most common in different disciplines. In this section, the evaluative potential of reporting verbs will be discussed. With an increased awareness of the evaluative potential of different reporting verbs you can assert your own voice in relation to the cited authors effectively by showing the degree of your support or agreement with the cited information. However, it is important to note that while the reporting verb does indeed carry evaluative potential, it is from the wider context in which the citations occur that an overall impression of writer voice can be gleaned.

Different reporting verbs can show the following:

- writer agreement with the cited author (e.g. show, find, point out);
- writer disagreement with or negative criticism of the cited author (e.g. omit, fail, miscalculate);
- a neutral writer view of the cited information (e.g. examine, discuss, explain, argue, contend, suggest).

When a writer indicates a neutral view using one of the reporting verbs from the latter group, it creates an expectation among the readers that he or she will he go on to either give his or her view in a later sentence or present an alternative or supporting point from another source.

The reporting verb can also indicate the strength of commitment of the cited author to his or her own opinion or finding. For example, 'suggested' and 'hypothesised' suggest caution on the part of the cited author.

Neutral reporting verbs

In Example 9.10, all the reporting verbs are neutral in the sense that they do not give away the writer's position. The reporting verbs, 'advocate', 'contend' and 'argue' indicate strong viewpoints on the part of the cited authors which are not universally agreed upon. Indeed, the reason why integral references are favoured here is the emphasis that they place on differing interpretations. The writer's comments on the strategies presented in the extract are made much later in the chapter in the conclusion, and they are not included as part of the illustration due to the length of the chapter and its conclusions. In relation to Table 9.1 above, this is an example of the writer's voice being 'delayed'.

Example 9.10 Neutral reporting verbs

eg → This section will review a set of US strategies of containment to illustrate that they had alternated between concepts of symmetrical and asymmetrical response to Communist encroachments in the face of structural and domestic constraints. For the advocates of asymmetrical response, such as Kennan, the Eisenhower administration (1953–61) and the Nixon administration (1969–74), the major policy instruments on hand were economic aid and nuclear deterrence. Conversely, the authors of NSC–68, the Kennedy administration (1961–3) and the Reagan administration (1981–9) advocated flexibility in mobilizing resources to act at all levels. Kissinger (1977) noted that the US approach to the world had oscillated between isolationism and overstretch and what was needed was a sense of realism to accept the world as given. Gaddis (1982) contended that the prime reason for these oscillations derived from internal forces operating within the United States, such as the Congress and the military–industrial complex, rather than the attitude or actions of the Soviet Union. Kaldor (1995) argued that the Cold War was an 'imaginary war' created by the leaders of the two competing blocs as part of their political strategies to divert public attention from domestic problems by spawning periodic threats.

Source: Son, 2004: 16–17

Reporting verbs which show writer agreement

Example 9.11 presents a section of a longer example already presented in Chapter 8 (Example 8.2b). The reporting verbs 'show' and 'found' indicate writer agreement with the findings of the cited authors. However, it is significant to note that in the next paragraph the writer introduces a critique of these studies where a number of weaknesses are highlighted. Therefore, the evaluative potential of reporting verbs can only be fully interpreted by examining the wider context.

Example 9.11 Reporting verbs showing writer agreement

eg → Correlational studies show that intentions are reliably associated with behaviour. A meta-analysis of 10 meta-analyses by Sheeran (2002) found that, based on 422 studies and a sample size of 82,107, intentions accounted for 28% of the variance in behaviour (r+= .53). In the context of the Theory of Planned Behaviour (TPB), Armitage and Connor's (2001) meta-analysis of 185 studies found that intentions accounted for 22% of the variance in behaviour (r+= .47). Calculation of fail-safe N indicated that 26,235 studies showing that intentions are not predictive of behaviour would be required in order to be able to conclude that intention has no significant relationship with behaviour (for similar findings, see meta-analyses by Ajzen, 1991; Godin & Kok, 1996; Hausenblas, Carron, & Mack, 1997; van den Putte, 1991).

However, a number of problems are encountered when attempting to infer causation from correlational studies.

Source: Webb, 2003: 3

TABLE 9.2 Linguistic strategies to show different degrees of commitment

Showing strong commitment	Showing agreement	Showing cautious commitment
From the sources in the 1500s, *it is clear* that ...	The following issues *demonstrate* that ...	Hancock *hypothesises* that ...
In summary, *it is beyond doubt* that ...	The examples given earlier *show* ...	On a larger scale, these discussions *suggest* ...
Hence, it does not come as a surprise that ...	Todd (1990) provides a *useful* approach to ...	
Aptly, Smythe (2005) emphasised how ...	This definition of sustainability is *more comprehensive* because...	
To date, the *strongest* argument against punitive measures is made by ...		

Evaluative adjectives, adverbs and phrases

There are a number of ways that you can show your strength of commitment to both unattributed statements that you make and to the citations included on your work. You can show that you strongly support an idea or alternatively that you are cautious or tentative in your belief in a point. The linguistic devices that you can draw on to do this include adjectives (e.g. strong, weak) and adverbs (e.g. undoubtedly, forcefully), the comparative and superlative forms of adjectives and adverbs (e.g. better, best; weaker, weakest; more smoothly, most smoothly, least smoothly), phrases (e.g. it is clear that ...; it is doubtful whether ...), and tentative verbs (e.g. suggest; hypothesise; propose).

The examples in Table 9.2 are grouped into three categories in which the writer shows: 1) a strong commitment to or agreement with the cited material; 2) agreement with the citation but it is less emphatic than in the group 1 examples; or 3) cautious commitment to the cited information. In each group, a range of linguistic strategies is illustrated.

Example 9.12, taken from Key-young's thesis, shows the use of evaluative words in context: 'appropriate' and 'indispensable'. He shows strong commitment to the 'constructivist approach'. In Example 9.13, Hannah uses the adverb 'convincingly' to acknowledge the strength of the cited author's argument.

Example 9.12 Evaluative adjectives showing support

eg → Hence, the appropriate use of a constructivist approach, which is keen to identify clues to historical change, is indispensable in order to conceptualize comprehensive engagement.

Source: Son, 2004: 54

Example 9.13 Evaluative adverbs showing support

eg → Lee (2001) argues convincingly that the credibility of the dominant framework, with its standard views of adulthood and dependent childhood, was supported by the socioeconomic and political climate of the early twentieth century.

Source: Fairbrother, 2010: 6

See Examples 8.1a and 9.4 for additional examples of the use of evaluative adjectives.

A mixture of evaluative strategies

In the final example, 9.14, a number of the approaches for foregrounding writer voice noted in this chapter are illustrated. The extract is taken from a section in the literature review of a dissertation from recreation and leisure studies. Dawn's dissertation discusses issues related to employee commitment to their organisations. I include a brief explanation after the example of the various ways that Dawn asserts her own voice in her writing.

Example 9.14 A variety of ways of foregrounding writer voice

 Importance of commitment

Committed employees contribute greatly to organizations because they perform and behave with a view to achieving organizational goals (Sutano 1999). Furthermore, commitment to organizations has been found to be positively related to such organizational outcomes as job satisfaction, motivation and attendance (Bennett and Durkin, 2000). On the other hand, the negative effects associated with a lack of organizational commitment include absenteeism and labour turnover (Bennett and Durkin, 2000). These examples help to demonstrate that workers who are committed to their organization are happy to be members of it. Therefore, employees who believe in the organization and are dedicated to what it stands for, intend to do what is good for the organization. This attitudinal approach reflects the nature and quality of the linkage between an employee and an organization. Oliver (1990) explains this employee–organization relationship in terms of the principle of exchange. Exchange theory is relevant to the attitudinal approach to commitment in that it is reasoned that employees offer commitment in return for the receipt (or anticipated receipt) of rewards from the organization. This view offers a simple way to think about the underlying motivations for why employees behave the way they do towards an organization. Using Oliver's reasoning it can be hypothesised, for the purpose of illustrating the importance of commitment, that when an organization exerts effort to improve the characteristics that influence commitment among employees, then employees will exert more effort to achieve the organization's goals. This is because they are receiving the quality personal, role-related, structural and job experiences that greatly contribute to improving organizational commitment.

Source: Culverson, 2002: 30–1

In the first three sentences of the extract, using non-integral references, Dawn strategically attributes different pieces of information to different sources in order to develop a comprehensive argument. The use of non-integral references enables her to control the direction of the text. She explicitly highlights the relationship between the citations with the connectors 'Furthermore' and 'On the other hand'.

Dawn foregrounds her own voice when she introduces her own comments and evaluation of the preceding citations with the phrase 'These examples help to demonstrate'. Her subsequent two sentences continue in the same vein, beginning with 'Therefore' and 'This attitudinal approach reflects …'.

She includes one neutral integral reference to Oliver with the reporting verb 'explains' and then goes on to elaborate on how she is drawing on the citation which she signals by the phrases 'This view offers ...' and 'Using Oliver's reasoning ...'. The use of the integral reference, 'Oliver (1990) *explains* ...', serves to emphasise her acknowledgement of Oliver for the theory of exchange but with the subsequent elaboration on this theory she clearly takes ownership of how the idea integrates with her own research interests. She is careful to show cautious commitment and not overstate her claims with the phrase 'it can be hypothesized'.

In this short extract from a literature review, we can see how a writer can direct the text for her own purposes and at the same time include citations to support her argument.

Task 9.1 Reflecting on the writer's voice in your own research

Take a paragraph or section that you have written for your own literature review and consider the following questions and suggestion.

Whose voice do you think is more dominant in your writing: your own or that of the authors you are citing?

Why do you think this is the case?

Do you feel you achieve a successful balance between your own voice and that of the authors whose work you cite?

If you believe it would improve your writing, try some of the techniques suggested in this chapter either to assert your own voice more strongly, or to substantiate your views more comprehensively by including additional references to the work of others.

 Summary

In this chapter we have considered the meaning of and reasons for 'foregrounding writer voice', and a range of strategies and examples which show how this can be achieved, namely:

- the strategic organisation of the text;
- the use of personal pronouns;
- the choice of citation pattern;
- exploiting the evaluative potential of different reporting verbs;
- the use of evaluative adjectives, adverbs and phrases.

10

The continuing process

Chapter summary

In this chapter, we discuss:

- the continuous process involved in the creation of the literature review;
- the integration of the literature when discussing the findings of your research.

The literature review process

As emphasised in both Chapters 1 and 6, the literature review process is a continuous one which begins when you first start to develop an idea for your research and does not end until the final draft of the dissertation or thesis is complete. Throughout the book, we have highlighted that the ongoing nature of the literature review is an integral part of the research process, because your work is always interconnected with that of others. For this reason, it is important that you are continually exploring the related developments in your field and that you keep reading as new publications appear which may be relevant to your research. As time goes by, it is possible that you will come across different theories, methodologies and ideas which cause you to see your own research in a different light. These references will then need to be integrated into your writing in later drafts of your literature review.

You may also wish to revise your literature review in the light of your own research findings. It may be that your research generates certain results which cause you to change the focus of your literature review or even to introduce and discuss an area of reading that you had not included previously. Finally, it is important to mention again that it is through the redrafting of your literature review that you are able to fine-tune your arguments, and clarify and articulate the focus of your research and the research questions.

The following quotes are from the writers of some of the dissertations and theses from which extracts have appeared throughout this book. They describe what the literature review process means to them.

My reading gradually broadened out from a narrow base, as I looked up references in articles/books I read. Sometimes I returned to original sources for more in-depth information. The more I read, the better it all fitted together, and it linked back to undergraduate research on other topics so gradually, it became part of my 'overall world view'. In terms of writing the dissertation, the lit review took longer than anything else! As I read more, I could edit out bits no longer necessary/relevant. This took a long time, and I found it quite challenging. However, the benefits of having done all the reading paid off in my dissertation, as well as in my working life. I feel I have a serious understanding of the subject, and it has built my confidence enormously. My research was based on educational e-learning projects, so I had the 'working knowledge' of the subject before I had the literature 'underpinning'. It helped validate what I had learned in practice.

Claire Allam, MEd Education

Given the primarily practical nature of my dissertation, the original focus of the literature review did not change greatly during the writing process. At the onset, I focused on three main areas: a general background to the position of pronunciation in English Language teaching, the effects of instruction on learning and the specific features of pronunciation under consideration in the study.

The most obvious change in focus came from the fairly general reading which accompanies early research to the more specific reading which becomes necessary as ideas and focus are refined. For example, while reading about the position of pronunciation within language teaching, it quickly became apparent that I needed more information on what kind of pronunciation model was desirable for students. This in turn led to needing information on the notion of 'comfortable intelligibility' and accepted definitions of the concept.

With respect to the effects of instruction on learning, I began by reading easily available books about general theories of Second Language Acquisition (SLA). This helped me to provide evidence that instruction appears to facilitate learning. The majority of research, however, focused on general learning rather than the specific learning of pronunciation. Through some of the reading I did, I found references to articles about other studies which were of interest. In addition I used ERIC and ATHENS extensively to search for relevant articles which were ordered from the British Library (I was working in Germany at the time and had limited access to libraries).

Analeen Moore, Education and Applied Linguistics

Writing a PhD dissertation is like swimming in an ocean-size pool full with a variety of different marine life. You need to sort out them in accordance with the differences and similarities. Most of all, it is important to find a niche habitat for your own PhD or restructure the whole ecosystem of the pool, if you can. Since a student starts from scratch, it is normal to revise the original literature review in the course of doing research. In many cases, the aims and objectives are shifting over time, a development which makes the student change the focus of his or her literature review. At the end of the day, it is just a process of building a solid and coherent foundation prior to making the main arguments in the next chapters.

Key-young Son, PhD East Asian Studies

I must confess that my literature review was written in the final few months of my PhD. My PhD was done before the requirement that students write a literature review in the first year. Thus, I focused my time on writing papers (with specific literature reviews to complement the data being presented) and then wrote the overall literature review for the thesis by drawing from these.

Having said this, I agree with the argument that the literature review is often revised in the light of data collection. In fact, so much so that I have given up trying to write an introduction to a paper before I have the data. I usually start with the method and results sections, then write the introduction, then the discussion.

Tom Webb, PhD Psychology

Referring to the literature in your discussion chapter

When reaching the 'Discussion' sections or chapter/s of your dissertation or thesis where you interpret your research findings, it is important to revisit the literature to contextualise your work again within the wider field of study. At both the beginning and end of your thesis or dissertation, your reader must be able to see how your research is rooted in and contributes to the ongoing development of knowledge in your field.

At this point in your thesis or dissertation, it is helpful to remind your reader about the content of your literature review. This could entail a summary of the main points or you could refer back to the literature discussed in earlier sections and chapters, providing cross-references for your readers.

When interpreting your own research findings, citations can be integrated to compare and contrast your findings with those of previous studies. It is important to point out how your work either supports or contradicts related previous work in your field. The literature may also provide a way for you to interpret your findings. A particular theory might provide a framework for your data analysis and interpretation. Alternatively, your data analysis may enable you to propose an amendment or development of a theory in your field.

Examples 10.1 to 10.7 illustrate these purposes for including references to the work of others in the discussion chapter/s of the dissertation or thesis. The italicised parts of the texts indicate how and where the writers make connections and show relationships between their research findings and the related literature.

Findings support an existing theory

In Example 10.1, taken from the masters dissertation on the relationship between pronunciation instruction and learning of pronunciation among English as a Foreign Language students, Analeen discusses the extent to which her results support Krashen's hypotheses on language learning and acquisition. Note the first sentence of the section, which reminds the reader about the purpose of the study.

Example 10.1 Findings support an existing theory

Discussion

eg → Effect of Instruction on Specific Features of Pronunciation and General Intelligibility

This study was designed to investigate the effect of instruction on pronunciation performance for learners at an elementary level of English. Given the time restrictions on the study, an elementary level was chosen so that there was not too much phonological fossilisation present in the sample and greater improvement could be expected from each learner than with a more advanced level sample where phonological fossilisation may have been greater.

It is interesting to note that both groups displayed improved pronunciation skills at the end of the study. Given that the control group received no instruction, this suggests that pronunciation skills are improved by exposure to the target language in the classroom. The control group appears to have noticed features of the phonological system and this has produced improvement. *This would seem to support Krashen's theory (1982) of exposure to TL at a level of (i + 1) producing acquisition* because in the classroom a teacher monitors their use of language and new items introduced. Therefore it would be hoped that a large amount of input is provided at a level suitable for the students to acquire it. The findings of the t-tests on the post-test results indicate that there was a positive relationship between instruction and the production of specific features of pronunciation but not between instruction and overall general intelligibility. *This would seem to confirm* Krashen's hypothesis that instruction produces learning but not acquisition since the learners were able to use what they had learnt when focusing on form, but they did not transfer it to their spontaneous speech when the focus was on meaning.

It is important to consider the listener-raters in relation to the results here. Despite the fact that the correlations between raters were very high indicating reliability, it may be the case that rating sentences is easier than assessing general intelligibility. When rating a sentence the rater is looking for a particular feature and the number of possible errors is limited. Spontaneous speech, in contrast, may contain many errors in areas such as grammar, phonology, fluency and discourse. The rater may be affected by a combination of these errors when making a judgment and thus not fairly represent just the subject's phonological intelligibility. A further complication may have arisen due to the fact that all raters are used to German learners' pronunciation of English, which may have influenced their perception of pronunciation performance. The raters may have penalised the subjects for making typical German pronunciation errors which did not impede intelligibility, or they may have not penalised the subjects for errors which could cause problems with intelligibility for those not used to German learners pronunciation of English. It might have been better to include some non-specialist raters so that any possible influence could have been controlled for. *For these reasons, it is not possible from this study to provide clear evidence* supporting Krashen's hypotheses of instruction only producing learning and not acquisition.

Source: Moore, 2001: 31–2

Comparing a new model and an existing theory

In Example 10.2, taken from a discussion section of a Psychology PhD thesis, Tom describes a theory (the factor model) which he has developed from his data analysis and compares it with a theory (model of action phases) previously discussed in his literature review. As in Example 10.1, observe the way the introductory sentence in the section reminds the reader of the focus of the research studies.

Example 10.2 A comparison between a new model and existing theory

General Discussion

eg → Studies 2 and 3 provide an important analysis of both the conceptual structure of constructs from goal theories and their relative importance in predicting goal attainment. Both retrospective (Study 2) and prospective (Study 3) designs provided evidence that five factors – motivation, task focus, implementation intentions, social support, and subjective norm – distinguish when people succeed in achieving personal goals from when they fail. This discussion will consider the implications of the factor model for the distinction between motivational and volitional processes and then the predictive effects.

The factor structure supports the model of action phases (Heckhausen, 1987; Heckhausen & Gollwitzer, 1986; 1987, see Section 1.2). The first factor – motivation – embraced concepts relating to goal selection; intention, commitment, and attitude toward the goal (perceived utility). *Thus, the first factor neatly parallels* the predecisional phase of action, which consists of deliberating wishes and setting preferences (Gollwitzer, 1990). *The factor structure also supports* the distinction between the predecisional (goal setting) and preactional (planning) phases of action – variables measuring implementation intentions were distinct from motivational constructs. Notably, in Study 3 items measuring acquiescence negatively loaded on the implementation intentions factor which suggests that the opposite of forming a plan is 'letting things slide' and 'not making things happen'. The model of action phases *also acknowledges* that achieving a personal goal is not simply about initiation of the relevant behaviour, but also requires maintenance of the behaviour over time. Thus, the actional phase refers to ideas of goal striving that *parallel* the present conception of task focus. For example, goal striving requires that one 'puts energy into the task' and 'does not allow thoughts to wander.' *In sum, the identified factor structure discriminates between constructs that influence behaviour at different phases in the course of action.*

Source: Webb, 2003: 84–5

Explaining a finding using the literature

In Example 10.3, which comes from the same section of the psychology thesis as the previous example, Tom uses the literature to support his explanations as to why a particular factor (self-efficacy) was not a distinguishing one between successful or failed attempts to achieve a goal. Note how Tom, in the first two sentences, makes a connection between the material that has been previously discussed and the discussion that is going to follow. This is an example of a smooth and effective transition in the text.

Example 10.3 Using the literature to help explain a finding

eg → The discussion thus far has focused on the five factors that discriminated successful from failed attempts to achieve personal goals. However, findings pertaining to factors that failed to distinguish the groups also merit discussion. It is notable that self-efficacy did not discriminate between participants who failed and participants who succeeded. *One explanation for this finding* is that self-efficacy may influence performance through the selection of personal goals, rather than influencing goal striving itself (Locke & Latham, 1990). For example, people are unlikely to try to achieve behavioural targets over which they feel they have little control (Bandura & Wood, 1989; Earley & Lituchy, 1991; Gibbons & Weingart, 2001). *Alternatively*, self-efficacy could have influenced goal achievement indirectly through task focus. For example, there is evidence to suggest that high self-efficacy leads to greater focus on the task whereas low self-efficacy directs attention to self-evaluation and increases self-doubt (Gibbons & Weingart, 2001). *In sum, self-efficacy may not have affected performance directly because* its effects were mediated by the selection of personal goals and/or task focus.

Source: Webb, 2003: 87–8

Contribution of current research to existing theory

In Example 10.4, from East Asian Studies, Key-young discusses the contribution of his research to the theoretical debates in the field of international relations. After reiterating the limitations of realism and liberalism, he explains how his research has extended the role of constructivism in the field by using it to analyse the specific context on the Korean Peninsula between 1998 and 2003.

Example 10.4 The current research contributes to existing theory

Contributions to theory

International Relations (IR) is rich in terms of the amount of literature on diverse features of international life. The works of theorists in this field, however, deal with similar subjects, war and peace, or conflicts and cooperation, but come up with diametrically opposed positions and interpretations. In spite of the abundance in terms of quantity, IR theories suffer from poverty mainly because of their incommensurability (Wight 1996). Realism witnessed its heyday for half a century between 1939 and 1989, a period marked by World War II, the Cold War and localized conflicts. Nevertheless, realism has somewhat lost its predictive and descriptive power with the end of the Cold War and the Soviet Union's voluntary retreat from its Cold War status (Kegley 1995: 7). As part of efforts to overcome the discipline's polarization and incommensurability, the neo-realists and neo-liberals formed the so-called 'neo-neo partnership', but fell short of formulating a grand theory, which can be called a paradigm.

Against this backdrop of inter-paradigm debates, constructivism emerged, seemingly invalidating decades of debates between the established theoretical schools. Constructivists claimed that another round of debate had begun between positivism and post-positivism, dismissing all past dialogues between realists, liberals and Marxists as positivist ones (Wight 1996). Constructivism imbued IR students with new ideas and tools that showed the potential for explaining the complex world of international politics. The new tools of constructivists, comprising such ideational factors as identities and norms, were potent weapons to explain the underlying forces of continuities and transformations. Nevertheless, constructivism 'remains more of a philosophically and theoretically informed perspective on and approach to the empirical study of international relations' than a full-fledged theory (Ruggie 1998: 856).

Therefore, this dissertation aimed to sharpen the constructivist approach to international relations and *formulate a testable hypothesis* in the field of strategies of engagement. *In particular, this dissertation discovered* the necessary conditions and social settings for the shift of a state's identity vis-à-vis an enemy state *and explained* what kinds of tools an activist government could mobilize in engaging an enemy state to implement strategies of comprehensive engagement. *Having analyzed a set of case studies, this research demonstrated that* a constructivist approach is able to play a significant role in supplementing 'problem-solving theories' in times of momentous change. *By formulating* the identity norm life cycle, which is an historically grounded conceptual framework, *this dissertation demonstrated that* a given government, in this case South Korea, which finds itself somewhere on the friendship–enmity continuum, is able to act as a norm entrepreneur in order to successfully resolve the conflicts of interests with an enemy state, a dimension that was not addressed by the theories of realism and liberalism.

Source: Son, 2004: 359–60

Interpreting the data using the literature

In the first paragraph of Example 10.5, Ei leen Lee refers back to a theory discussed in the literature review and explains how it has influenced her data analysis of the shift in language use of the Creole being studied. In the latter paragraph included in the extract, she introduces the concept of 'negotiation' to assist in the interpretation of her data.

Example 10.5 Using the theory to interpret the data

From the Findings and Conclusions (Chapter 8)

In Chapter 2, three main approaches to the study of language shift (LS) in minority communities were discussed, namely investigating LS through domains, through

(Continued)

(Continued)

behaviour and through bilingualism. The theoretical constructs underlying the approaches are drawn from sociology, social psychology, and bilingualism respectively. *The review of these approaches demonstrates that* the LS of [the Creole] needs to be studied, analysed and understood through an eclectic approach drawing from an interdisciplinary perspective as the language behaviour of the speakers which is directing the LS of [the Creole] is brought about not by one but [by] an interdependence of these factors.

...

Most studies of negotiation apply to the field of corporate conflict resolution and the term describes a problem-solving encounter between parties who each have their own agenda and goals. According to Firth (1995: 10), in many cases, 'negotiation is used metaphorically to stress that the essential nature of a phenomenon is not stasis or fixity but its contingent mutability, its situated emergence, and its intersubjective interpretation ... '. As human interactions are not predetermined or fixed entities, the concept of negotiation has been applied to the interactional and pragmatic use of language such as the studies on context (e.g. Kendon, 1999), turn-taking (e.g. Fairclough, 1992) and topics (e.g. Gumperz, 1982), to name a few. In most of these studies the concept of negotiation applies to how the parties concerned make an ongoing assessment of the situation to make the appropriate 'move'. In the case of LS and revitalisation of [the Creole], *I would like to extend the concept of negotiation to refer to* [the Creole] speakers' ongoing assessment of what is most important to their situation and how these priorities are manifested in their language choice, language use, attitude and response to the shift and revitalisation of [the Creole].

Source: Lee, 2003: 325–7

Application of theory to the findings

In her literature review, Ling discussed three curriculum perspectives (socially critical, liberal progressive and postmodern), which she used to provide the theoretical framework for her research. She conducted three HE case studies in China and the UK, focusing on the curricula for education for sustainable development. In the first part of her discussion chapter, she compares how the three case study HE institutions engaged with each of the curriculum perspectives, thereby linking back to the literature cited earlier in the thesis. In the extract below, she begins to discuss socially-critical education for sustainable development and how it is realised in the three case study curricula. In this extract, she provides explicit cross-references back to the literature review chapter.

Example 10.6 Connecting the theory with the findings

 Socially-critical sustainability education and the three curricula

With regards to how the three curricula applied aspects of socially-critical sustainability education (Saha 2002; Thomas 2005; Plant 2001), the research findings show that only Course A was generally committed to and applied socially-critical sustainability education; two out of three Course B staff interviewees explicitly expressed their disagreement with socially-critical sustainability education, but one aspect of socially-critical sustainability education – critical thinking – was adopted by Course B in a pragmatic fashion; Course C adopted one aspect of socially-critical sustainability education – 'action-orientation' without explicitly linking this with socially-critical sustainability education.

TABLE 7   Key characteristics of the three curricula that reflected socially-critical sustainability education

	Course A	Course B	Course C
Socially-critical sustainability education: key characteristics	explicitness of values and positions, transformative learning and action-orientation	critical thinking	action-orientation

Firstly, both Courses A and C contained a key curriculum characteristic I called 'action-orientation'; however, 'action' meant different things in the two curricula: through transformative learning, Course A encouraged students to identify political and social actions that could contribute to social change towards SD with a focus on social justice and democratisation whereas Course C encouraged students to plan and implement feasible and practical actions mainly in the context of Chinese schools. Both types of 'action-orientation' were commented on favourably by students on both courses.

Before asking the question what the courses can learn from each other in the socially-critical sustainability education framework, it is important to analyse the social and political backgrounds of 'action-orientation' in England and China. The politically radical curriculum of Course A was enabled by the relative institutional autonomy and academic freedom of English HEIs (Department for Education and

(Continued)

(Continued)

Skills, 2003) (see Section 2.5.1) … On the other hand, Course C was operating in the more restrictive intellectual environment of Chinese HE, as I have discussed in section 2.5.2.

Source: Feng, 2010:179–80

Highlighting an unexpected result

In Example 10.7, extracted from the discussion of results in an engineering thesis, the writer presents an unexpected result in relation to previous work in the field. He then draws an overall conclusion beginning with the phrase, 'It appears'.

Example 10.7 A surprising finding in relation to previous research

eg → Several important ideas resulting from the microcosm work have now been considered at the field scale. Transferring the microcosm model to field scale has resulted in a new fully-kinetic, two-step syntrophic biodegradation model for plumes. This model has generally reproduced observed detailed MLS (multi-level sampler) profiles at a field site, and the pattern of concomitant TEAPs (Terminal electron accepting processes) in the plume core. In examining the similarities and differences between the laboratory and field case, it has been important to have a consistent conceptual framework, yet with flexibility to include differing parameter values as required by the different cases, and the fully kinetic model has met these needs. It was found that while the microcosm conceptual reaction model was transferable to the field scale, the value of the rate parameters were not, since the reactions are much slower in the field.

In both field and laboratory cases, the microbial activities of both fermenters and TEAPs change with time, and space, due to processes such as growth, bioavailability, acclimatisation, and toxic effects. An important result of considering acclimatisation, and consequent increase of rates with exposure time, is that the core reactions turned over more contaminant mass than the fringe reactions, *which was not expected from former studies of the plume* (Mayer et al. 2001; Thornton et al. 2001). It appears, in general, that reactive transport models used for NA (natural attenuation) assessment should consider such temporal and spatial changes.

Source: Watson, 2004: 69

Task 10.1 Reflecting on making the connections in your own research

When interpreting the findings from your own research, for example in the discussion chapter of your dissertation or thesis, consider how you make connections with the related literature from your field. Have you done any or all of the following?

1   Have you referred back to a literature review chapter presented earlier in the dissertation or thesis by, for example:
    * summarising the main points from your literature review?
    * reminding your reader of the content of your literature review with a cross-reference (e.g. 'In Chapter two, there was an overview of local authority policies on recycling')?

2   Have you compared your findings with those of similar research projects in your field?

3   Have you drawn on a particular theory or theories in your field through which to interpret your findings?

4   Have you shown how your findings have shed new light on professional practice or theory in your field?

Summary

To summarise, this chapter has considered:

* the ongoing process of a literature review;
* the significance of revisiting the literature when discussing the research findings.

11

A systematic literature review

Chapter summary

This chapter discusses:

- the meaning of a systematic literature review and how it differs from a dissertation or thesis literature review;
- the process of doing a systematic literature review;
- different approaches to the analysis and synthesis of data: meta-analysis and narrative synthesis
- a checklist of questions for the critical appraisal of a systematic literature review.

What is a systematic literature review?

A systematic review is a literature review usually carried out by a group of experienced professionals which addresses clearly stated aims and/or research questions. Traditionally, systematic reviews examined the effectiveness of a healthcare intervention but more recently they have looked at wider issues such as how and why an intervention works, its feasibility, appropriacy and cost effectiveness. The aim is to synthesise research findings from a large number of different studies on a particular intervention or issue which can then potentially be used to inform policy and practice in the field investigated. The methods are made explicit so as to be replicable and these include a clear search strategy, inclusion and exclusion criteria for publications and studies selected from the search, a synthesis of data from the sources included and a detailed coding and analysis of the findings from all the studies. There is also likely to be input in the process from stakeholders, for example policy makers, and users of a service (the Campbell Collaboration; EPPI-Centre, 2007; Rutter et al., 2010; Jesson et al., 2011).

Typically a systematic review is commissioned by a government body or public service to inform decision making. Initially, reviews were introduced in the field of health in the 1970s and 1980s; these later came under the auspices of the Cochrane Collaboration (http://www.cochrane.org/), whose first centre was officially opened in Oxford in 1993 to oversee and offer guidance to those conducting reviews investigating the effectiveness of healthcare interventions. The Cochrane Collaboration has since developed into an international network of researchers and healthcare professionals involved in evidence-based medical and health related decisions. Subsequently, different groups such as the Campbell Collaboration (http://www.campbellcollaboration. org/), EPPI (Evidence-informed Policy and Practice Centre) (http://www.eppi. ioe.ac.uk), and SCIE (Social Care Institute for Excellence) (http://www.scie. org.uk) have all extended the use of systematic reviews to other fields including criminal justice, social care and welfare, education, and employment. All of these organisations have libraries of systematic reviews which can be accessed online. Their web sites also offer guidance on the process of conducting a systematic review and the range of methods and approaches to analysis and synthesis that can be used.

The need for systematic reviews in an ever wider range of fields has arisen from recognition of the importance of evidence based practice to inform policy decisions and professional practice. Before choices can be made, an overview has to be gained of all the evidence available and a rigorously conducted systematic review can provide this, preventing a situation where decisions are made on the basis of a single, possibly poor quality, study. Furthermore, the huge increase in the number of publications available, as the Internet has become the predominant means of information sharing, makes it impossible for an individual to read everything that is being published. Thus, systematic reviews can provide a synthesis of evidence on a specific issue which can be a great time saver for busy practitioners.

This type of review is clearly different from a dissertation or thesis literature review, which has been the main focus of this book so far. Nevertheless, an understanding of the role and nature of systematic literature reviews is important even if not undertaking one yourself. It is often relevant to consult systematic reviews on particular issues as part of a dissertation or thesis literature review. To recap on the differences between the two types, a literature review which is part of a research project involving the collection of primary data, e.g. a masters research dissertation, provides a context and theoretical underpinning to the research, evaluates related empirical studies, and identifies how the current project extends or fills a gap in previously reported research in the field. In contrast, a systematic literature review is in itself a research study, addressing research questions and using the literature as data to be coded, analysed and synthesised to reach overall conclusions. Many of the techniques and tools described in earlier chapters (e.g. literature searching, reading and note taking, reference management, citation practices) are applicable for both sorts of review but the underlying purposes of each type are very different.

The process of conducting a systematic literature review

The web sites of the organisations cited above all include detailed advice on the process of conducting a systematic literature review. A concise summary is given below although it is recommended that the above web sites are visited if more specific detail is required. If conducting a stand-alone literature review for a degree programme assignment (as mentioned in Chapter 1), some of these steps may also offer a useful framework.

1   When a general area of enquiry has been identified, a scoping activity of the literature available is conducted by doing key word searches on all relevant catalogues and databases and systematically recording results.
2   A protocol or plan for the systematic review can then be developed to ensure that the study is transparent and rigorously carried out. It will need to be approved by a committee if the review is being conducted for a particular organisation (e.g. the Campbell Collaboration). The protocol and should cover the following:

- the proposed title, aim and research questions;
- the review team members;
- an overview of the background context including relevant legislation and current debates;
- literature searching and screening methods including details on how records will be kept;
- inclusion and exclusion criteria for the articles to be used as part of the review;
- data extraction strategies, i.e. what categories will be used for extracting data from the articles (aim, location, sample size, methods, findings etc);
- data synthesis approaches, e.g. meta-analysis (synthesis of numerical results) and/or coding and narrative synthesis of qualitative data.
- stakeholder involvement and input in the review; when and in what ways interested parties will have a role (e.g. when deciding on the aims of the review).
- timetable for the whole process.

An updated and revised version of the protocol can become the methods part of the systematic review itself when this is written.

1   After the protocol has been agreed, a comprehensive search of the literature is conducted and detailed records of all key word searches, databases used, dates, and numbers of hits are kept. As well as electronic sources, print sources and grey literature are explored (see Chapter 3 for more on conducting searches and keeping records).

2   Inclusion and exclusion criteria to all the retrieved articles and publications are then applied. It is common practice to apply these criteria at two levels, first, after reading the title and abstract, and second, after reading the article in its entirety. All decisions made along with the reasons should be documented on an Excel spreadsheet or table. Specified criteria for inclusion and exclusion in the review may relate to a number of different aspects of an article such as its date of publication, location of the research, detail and type of methodology, identity and size of sample, the type of intervention or the data analysis method. For example in a systematic review on the effect of vitamin C intake on the occurrence and duration of common colds, studies were excluded if the dose of vitamin C was less than 0.2 grams per day and if no placebo group was used for comparison. The studies included were not restricted to those based on randomised controlled trials (RCTs) (Hemilä et al. 2007). RCTs are experiments where participants are randomly allocated to a control group or treatment group as part of an investigation into the effects of an intervention; these trials are very influential in decision making about the most effective treatments in healthcare.

3   Studies may also be excluded for poor quality or insufficient detail or relevance to the review questions, so critical and evaluative reading is important. A checklist of questions can be devised to help with these decisions (see questions to guide critical reading in Chapters 4 and 8).

4   After the articles selected for inclusion have been identified, the data extraction takes place (see section on a tabular comparison of source texts in Chapter 4). All the chosen literature sources are read and consistent data is recorded about each one. This could be done as Word tables, Excel spreadsheets or in NVivo (see Chapters 4 and 5). Examples of the criteria that might be recorded about each article are as follows: full reference of the article, country of origin, setting of the study, objective of the research, study design, details about participants, type of intervention, details of control group (Torgerson et al. 2006).

5   Following the data extraction from each source, the synthesis of evidence takes place. This is when connections are made between all the articles read to address the research questions of the review. This may include a narrative synthesis of qualitative data or a meta-analysis of quantitative data. The latter would include a tabular presentation of data and/or charts incorporating statistics as a meta-analysis involves a synthesis of numerical results from comparable studies to produce an overall statistic. (See sections below and the further reading list at the end of the chapter for suggestions and links to more information about meta-analysis and narrative synthesis in systematic literature reviews.)

6   A mixed method approach to reviewing is also possible. An example is outlined by Harden and Thomas (2005), who describe the methods they adopted in a systematic

review on the barriers and facilitators to healthy eating amongst young children. Their review included a quantitative meta-analysis of healthy eating intervention studies, qualitative coding using NVivo and a synthesis of studies exploring personal perspectives on the issue, and a final matrix where the two sets of findings were compared. This combination of techniques allows for the findings from different types of research study to be combined so as to address the research questions posed for a systematic review in a fully comprehensive manner.

7 Based on the synthesis of data, recommendations for practice are made and conclusions are drawn.

8 The quality of systematic reviews is supported through the peer review process, which takes place on the final draft of the review. This means that professional colleagues read and comment on the work and make a recommendation regarding its suitability for publication.

9 If the article is accepted for publication after peer review, the final step involves dissemination of the results and recommendations to stakeholders and professionals in the field through publication in journals and on web pages, and presentations at seminars and conferences.

10 Regular updates will be implemented of systematic reviews which are made available through the online libraries of organisations such as the Cochrane Collaboration. As part of this process, key word searches are conducted in appropriate databases for recent and relevant studies and any necessary updates to the data synthesis and recommendations for practice will be included in the review.

There are now a range of different approaches to data synthesis in systematic reviews and it is important that reviewers take into account the topic, purpose and question of the review, the type of primary research evidence available, and the methodological backgrounds and preferences of the reviewers when making decisions about the most appropriate choice for a particular review (Boaz et al. 2006). In the following two sections, the two most widely used alternatives are discussed, but as Boaz et al. (2006) demonstrate, drawing on five examples of reviews from a variety of fields, there are many ways of combining and/or varying these.

What is a meta-analysis?

The various organisations mentioned above focus on different types of review. For example, as already explained, the Cochrane Collaboration investigates healthcare and health policy interventions and assesses their benefits and drawbacks. They also conduct reviews of diagnostic tests for diseases. The reviews are usually quantitative and often based on randomised controlled trials (RCTs). The synthesis of data from such studies involves meta-analysis, which is a technique that combines the statistical results from a number of similarly conducted individual investigations to reach an overall result. The analysis assesses the 'outcome measure' or 'effect' of an intervention by combining statistics from comparable studies. It determines the direction and size of the effect and whether it is consistent or different across studies. This synthesis gives more strength to the assessment of the effectiveness of an intervention because it is a combined result from a number of different investigations and thus gives a more precise measure.

It is beyond the scope of this book, to consider the detailed statistical techniques that can take place in various types of meta-analysis. However, more details are available in the *Cochrane Handbook for Systematic Reviews of Interventions* (available from www.cochrane-handbook.org) and further reading is listed at the end of this chapter. Nevertheless, some general principles involved in the meta-analysis process are outlined briefly below.

Meta-analysis is most appropriate when the studies combined in the review have addressed the same or comparable questions, have had a similar design and intervention, have measured the same outcomes and have used comparable statistical techniques, i.e. the studies are homogenous. If any of these aspects of the studies are too dissimilar and diverse, meta-analysis may not be suitable, or it should be analysed using a 'random-effects model' in an appropriate statistical package (see below). Homogenous studies can be analysed using a 'fixed effect model' to calculate a 'mean outcome measure' from all the data using a statistical package such as RevMan (2008), the Cochrane Collaboration Review Manager. This measure can be assumed to be attributable to the intervention and be used to produce a 'pooled effect estimate' of the intervention (Higgins and Green 2011).

Different studies may have different weightings in the meta-analysis based on the quality of the individual trials carried out. Decisions on the weightings of individual studies involve evaluative judgments based on factors such as the number of participants or the precise nature of outcome measures. In some fields, there may be established scales for measuring the weighting that individual studies should have in a meta-analysis (e.g. Jadad et al. 1996); for reviews in other areas, however, these scales may need to be established on a review by review basis to take into account the particular range of studies included in a particular instance.

The internal validity of a meta-analysis is established through a 'risk of bias' assessment. This is required to show that the conclusions drawn from a study are trustworthy with regard to the intervention being studied and that the research question posed in the review protocol has indeed been answered. *The Cochrane Handbook* (Higgins and Green 2011) includes a table for assessing bias which includes the following categories: selection bias, performance bias, detection bias, attrition bias and reporting bias. Under these headings, the following questions should be addressed: To what extent is the allocation to a treatment group random and blind? To what extent are participants and researchers blind to the intervention that has been applied? To what extent are those measuring outcomes blind to which intervention has been applied? To what extent are attritions reported and accounted for? Have outcomes been reported selectively and if so, to what extent? Studies can be rated according to the responses to each of these questions. For example, in RCTs, there is deemed to be less likelihood of bias if allocation to treatment and control groups is random and blind.

Sensitivity analysis is a process which assesses the robustness of the overall result of the meta-analysis. It is a procedure which shows the extent to which the pooled effect measure varies if the meta-analysis is conducted a second time with one altered criterion in the data included, e.g. a change in the date of publication of the studies included, or exclusion of unpublished data. The reason for a sensitivity analysis is that some decisions in the systematic review process may have been somewhat arbitrary, for example, a decision about the age range of participants included in a review investigating care for the elderly. A sensitivity analysis is implemented to show whether the results are robust enough not to change greatly if the meta-analysis is conducted again with a variation in the age range (e.g. only including studies with participants over the age of 65 instead of studies with participants over the ages of 60). If the results remain consistent, it shows that they are not affected by potentially arbitrary decisions in the review process and therefore the results of the review as a whole can be viewed with more certainty. There is a range of different decision points in the review process (e.g. inclusion criteria for the studies, characteristics of the interventions, outcome measures, statistical methods chosen, etc.) that can give rise to a sensitivity analysis and these will vary between different systematic reviews.

The above assessments are important and applicable when the studies in a meta-analysis are homogenous. Nevertheless, heterogeneity amongst studies in a systematic review does exist, and needs to be considered with care. If studies are heterogeneous, one or more of the following differs between them: characteristics of participants, interventions or outcome measures (clinical heterogeneity); study design or risk of bias measurements (methodological heterogeneity). The presence of any of these aspects of heterogeneity can result in statistical heterogeneity, meaning that the statistic representing the intervention effect varies more than would be expected from random error. There are statistical techniques for addressing heterogeneity, such as 'random-effects analyses' which can be conducted in the statistical package RevMan (2008) mentioned above. In reviews where heterogeneity is too great for a statistical analysis, a qualitative approach known as narrative synthesis may be appropriate (Popay et al., 2006) for the processing of data from diverse studies (see section below).

Narrative synthesis

It is important to bear in mind that a meta-analysis is not synonymous with a systematic review as many reviews rely on studies which are not randomised control trials but are based on qualitative data and analysis. Systematic reviews may be predominantly narrative or descriptive or they may include narrative elements alongside a meta-analysis (Boaz et al., 2006). For example, the EPPI centre carries out a variety of types of systematic review in a wide range of subject areas. An example of a review question and a review title are given below which do not lend themselves to meta-analyses:

What strategies can be used by initial teacher training providers, trainees and newly qualified teachers to raise the attainment of pupils from culturally diverse backgrounds (Parker-Jenkins et al., 2004)?

A synthesis of research addressing children's, young people's and parents' views of walking and cycling for transport (Brunton et al., 2006).

Narrative synthesis is an approach which can be incorporated into the systematic review process and involves using text and words to present the 'stories' of the studies being reported (Popay et al., 2006). It is a process that can be particularly helpful for reviews which are addressing questions that are not looking at the effectiveness of interventions but instead at the factors (facilitators and barriers) that might influence successful implementation. Narrative synthesis can be used as either a supplement or an alternative to meta-analysis and, as mentioned above, it is also a helpful approach when the studies being reviewed are very diverse in nature and/or report on qualitative research.

The brief overview of the process below is based on the guidelines that were developed by Popay et al. (2006) with funding from the ESRC (the Economic and Social Research Council) methods programme. The guidelines themselves include two worked examples of the process of narrative synthesis and the use of its tools. First, they present a narrative synthesis of studies from a Cochrane Collaboration systematic review which investigated the effects of interventions promoting smoke alarm ownership and function. As the review had originally been based on a meta-analysis, a comparison is made between those results and the findings of the narrative synthesis (Popay et al., 2006). Further use of some of the narrative synthesis tools is demonstrated in a review of a selection of studies investigating the implementation of smoke alarm interventions (Popay et al., 2006; Arai et al., 2007).

The methods and tools suggested are intended to ensure transparency of the narrative synthesis procedure; it is recommended that reviewers work separately on different stages of the process and then compare their analyses and syntheses. These should then be presented as mutually agreed or 'transparently divergent' (Arai et al. 2007: 380). There are four important phases of narrative synthesis: theory development, preliminary synthesis, the exploration of relationships and the assessment of robustness of the review.

The first step recommended is the development of a preliminary theory of how, why and for whom an intervention works. The purpose of this is to provide a framework that can guide decisions about the review question and the studies to be reviewed, and to assist with the interpretation and applicability of the review findings. This explanatory theory could be derived from an initial reading of studies likely to be included in the review and previous systematic reviews on related topics. To give an example, Popay et al. (2006) put forward a theory in relation to the use of smoke alarms, suggesting that education on the risks of fire can lead to the acquisition of alarms, and that the cost of the alarms could be a barrier to their acquisition.

As part of the preliminary synthesis, the reviewers should first write a textual summary of each individual study, encompassing studies that are both included and excluded from the review. There should be an agreement about the order and type of information included in the summaries to give a consistent format. These can then be condensed into tables with comparable information about each study in corresponding columns, e.g. author/year, location of study, participants, intervention and significant factors related to implementation (see Chapter 4 for an example of tabular presentation). The studies should then be grouped or clustered according to criteria such as their research setting, study design, characteristics of participants, intervention type, outcome measures, or the factors that may affect implementation. Again, tabular presentation with agreed headings is recommended, e.g. clustering of studies according to location, focus, or population (Popay et al. 2006; Arai et al., 2007). Alongside the clustering, an inductive thematic analysis should be carried out to identify key concepts which feature in the studies. For example, Arai et al. (2007) identified barriers and levers in relation to the acquisition, installation and the continued use of smoke alarms which resulted from a thematic analysis of the included studies, and then presented these themes in a table. It is important that reviewers keep explicit accounts of how the thematic analysis is conducted to ensure the transparency and rigour expected in a systematic review.

Another tool that may be used in the preliminary synthesis stage is 'vote counting', which essentially tallies the number of each type of result in relation to an intervention or implementation factor, giving different weightings where appropriate. This technique could give an indication of patterns emerging from the results. For example, in the EPPI Centre systematic review on views of cycling and walking, the reviewers tallied the number of studies that mentioned the different barriers and facilitators; for instance, 12 studies mentioned dangerous traffic as a barrier to walking and/or cycling and ten studies gave environmental reasons as a facilitator (Brunton et al., 2006: 37)

The purpose of the next phase of a narrative synthesis, exploring relationships, is to investigate factors that might explain differences in the direction and degree of effect of an intervention amongst studies in the systematic review or differences in the barriers and facilitators to implementation of an intervention. First, heterogeneity amongst studies should be explored by examining, for example, the variation in interventions and the effect this may have had on the outcome; this can involve the identification of moderator variables or factors that may have influenced the effect of the intervention or the implementation. For example, in the review investigating the implementation of smoke alarms, the implementation in one study was thought to have been more successful because of the involvement of the community in decision making (Popay et al., 2006; Arai et al., 2007).

Visual techniques, such as idea webbing and concept mapping, can be useful for exploring key concepts and potential relationships amongst issues arising in studies investigating an intervention or implementation (see Chapter 4 on pattern notes and mind mapping software). Another suggested technique is reciprocal translation, where a reviewer explores whether a concept present in one study is evident in another, even if labelled differently in the latter study; e.g. the role of the landlord in smoke alarm installation appeared to be significant in one study and so was explored further in the other studies (Popay et al. 2006; Arai et al., 2007). As a final step in the exploring relationships phase, the synthesis of key concepts can be summarised in tabular form and a narrative 'story' can be told. An extract of the narrative from the smoke alarm implementation study is included below.

> ... Two aspects of implementation appear to affect the success or otherwise of the interventions .... The commitment of landlords is beneficial at all stages: by providing alarms free of charge, or to overcome tenants' fears about damage to property; ... Tenants' appropriate perception of their own risk of domestic fires ... is necessary but insufficient at two stages: to motivate acquisition ... and to achieve maintenance.

> Arai et al., 2007: 377–8

The final phase of a narrative synthesis involves assessing the robustness of the review. The EPPI Centre has issued guidelines for establishing the 'weight of evidence' of a study based on three criteria: methodological soundness, appropriateness of study design, and the relevance of the study to the review questions; on the basis of the extent to which a study meets these expectations, the reviewers make a composite assessment of the overall weight that a study carries. Any grading system used to do this must be explicitly described as well as how the weightings are applied to the overall results of the synthesis. Additional techniques for assessing robustness include a comparison of results with earlier related reviews; checking the results with the authors of the primary studies included in the review; and writing a critical reflection on the narrative synthesis process.

Having given a concise overview of two very different approaches to analysis and synthesis of systematic literature review data, in the next section, I describe an example which draws on both techniques.

An example of a systematic review

In some systematic reviews, more than one intervention is investigated. In these cases different meta-analyses and/or narrative syntheses may need to be undertaken between different pairs of comparisons. For example, in a Cochrane Collaboration review, Fernandez and Griffiths (2010) looked at different types of cleansing solutions for wounds; because of the heterogeneity amongst the studies included in the review, they undertook five different comparisons between different wound treatments. They compared tap water and no cleansing, tap water and a saline solution, distilled water and a saline solution, tap water and cooled boiled water, and tap water and any other solution. For the range of comparisons of cleansing solutions, Fernandez and Griffiths (2010) conducted analyses for different outcome categories. For example, when comparing the use of tap water with a saline solution, first, they compared the infection rates in two types of wound: acute and chronic. As secondary outcomes, they also compared the rate of wound healing, the cost of using the different cleansing solutions and patient views on the method they preferred. Hence, different meta-analyses and descriptive analyses were conducted for the various comparisons before the authors presented an overall discussion and conclusion based on the results of all of these towards to end of the review. For comparisons where there were studies with enough homogeneity, they conducted a meta-analysis. For example, data from three RCTs were synthesised to compare cleansing with tap water and no cleansing which led to a meta-analysis that showed that there was no difference in infection rates between the two sample groups (Fernandez and Griffiths 2010: 6). For some of the secondary outcome measures, such as patient satisfaction there was a narrative synthesis of the data:

> a feeling of well being was reported ... among the patients who were allowed to shower their wounds.
>
> Fernandez and Griffiths, 2010: 6

Some further characteristics of systematic reviews are illustrated in relation to this example below.

Cochrane reviews include both an abstract and a plain language summary before the presentation of the detailed systematic review. The abstract contains a summary of the background and objectives of the review, the searches undertaken, the inclusion criteria for the synthesised studies, the data extraction and analysis methods, the statistical and descriptive findings of the review, as well as the authors' conclusions. The plain language summary is intended for a more general audience. An example of the latter for the wound cleansing review is included below; it illustrates the overall conclusions reached after the series of comparisons of cleansing solutions in relation to the various outcome measures:

The effects of water compared with other solutions for wound cleansing

Water is frequently used for cleaning wounds to prevent infection. This can be tap water, distilled water, cooled boiled water or saline (salty water). Using tap water to cleanse acute wounds in adults does not increase the infection rate; however, there is no strong evidence that cleansing per se is better than not cleansing. The reviewers concluded that where tap water is high quality (drinkable), it may be as good as other methods such as sterile water or saline (salty) water (and more cost-effective), but more research is needed (Fernandez and Griffiths 2010, p.2).

As mentioned above, reviews include information on the databases searched and key words used on each database. For example, the databases searched for a 2010 update of this review were:

Cochrane Wounds Group Specialised Register (Searched 22/2/10);
The Cochrane Central Register of Controlled Trials (CENTRAL) (The Cochrane Library, 2010 Issue 1);
Ovid MEDLINE – 2007 to February Week 2 2010;
Ovid MEDLINE – In-Process & Other Non-Indexed Citations (Searched 19/2/10);
Ovid EMBASE – 2007 to 2010 Week 06;
EBSCO CINAHL – 2007 to February 22 2010

Key word searches such as the following were used: (clean* or wash* or irrigat* or shower* or bath* or rins*) (Fernandez and Griffiths 2010, pp. 3–4)

Inclusion criteria for the articles used were: randomised controlled trials and quasi RCTs comparing effects of different cleansing solutions on healing and infection rates of wounds; trials undertaken in any country and in any language; trials with participants of all ages and from a range of different settings (e.g. hospitals, nursing homes etc); trials which compared solutions specifically intended for wound cleansing; trials which included both objective and subjective measures of wound infection and healing.

Exclusion criteria were the following: trials which looked at solutions used for dental procedures, burns, ulcers, operative procedures, or as a prophylactic, and trials which did not use tap water (Fernandez and Griffiths 2010, p. 3).

As part of the data extraction process, details from all the articles accessed and read were entered onto a table with the following headings: methods used in the study, characteristics of participants and wounds, interventions, the outcomes measured, notes about follow up to the treatment, and allocation concealment to the different groups involved the trial (an indicator of risk of bias). All the tables of the 11 included studies in the review appeared after the main body of the report. A second table listed the excluded studies with reasons given (Fernandez and Griffiths 2010, pp. 13–20).

Detailed tables were also included after the main report showing details of the various comparisons conducted with information about the number of studies involved, sample sizes, risk ratios and the size of the effect of each intervention on the different outcome measures. These were followed by charts which illustrated the statistics used for the corresponding meta-anlayses (Fernandez and Griffiths 2010, pp. 21–5).

Appendices of the review included further details which along with the above information on included and excluded studies and data analyses, ensured transparency of the systematic review process. In this example, there were: records of all databases and key words used in literature searches; reviewers comments and author responses; updates to the review; and details of the contributions of the individual authors to the systematic review as a whole (Fernandez and Griffiths 2010, pp. 25–30).

On the basis of this documentation, a practitioner considering whether to draw on the findings of this systematic review can assess the rigour with which the study has been conducted and evaluate whether the strength of evidence is enough to assist in any decision making about professional practice.

Appraisal of a systematic literature review

The evaluation of Internet sources and critical reading has been discussed in earlier chapters of the book. In a similar way, it is important to approach reviews with an open mind and adopt a questioning approach to their content and quality. Although the peer review process described above is intended to ensure that quality is maintained, as with all journal articles, books and web pages, it is important to make your own judgements. The following questions provide a checklist for a critical appraisal.

- Is the scope of the review clearly defined with appropriate research questions?
- Is there enough detail on the search strategies used? Which databases and types of sources were accessed? Was the search far reaching enough?
- Are the inclusion and quality criteria for the literature sources clearly given? Were they applied appropriately with more than one reviewer involved?
- Are the categories for extraction of data from each source explicit? Have they been consistently and appropriately applied by more than one reviewer?
- Is the process of analysis, whether quantitative or qualitative, explicit? Are any weightings used for different studies in a review and quality checks clearly explained? Does the

synthesis of evidence accurately reflect the findings from the individual studies and address the research questions posed at the start of the review?

- Are the recommendations in the review plainly based on the evidence from the systematic review synthesis of data?
- Has the review been peer reviewed and published by a recognised organisation or journal (e.g. The Cochrane Collaboration)?

Task 11.1 Searching for and critiquing a systematic literature review in your field

1   Make a note of any libraries of systematic reviews or journals which publish systematic reviews in your field; consider setting up RSS feeds or email alerts to receive up-to-date information on relevant new publications if the library or journal offers either or both of these facilities.
2   Search for a systematic literature review which could be relevant for your research. Conduct a key word search in an appropriate online library of systematic reviews (e.g. from the EPPI Centre or Cochrane Collaboration web pages) or on Google scholar, search for 'Systematic literature review *key words of your choice*'.
3   After selecting and accessing a review, use skimming strategies (Chapter 3) to assess its relevance for your work.
4   If it is of interest, read the review in more detail, take notes using your preferred technique and apply the critical appraisal questions above.
5   Decide on whether and how you can draw on the findings of the systematic literature review for your own research.
6   Identify any cited studies in the review that you feel are important to access yourself as a primary source of information.

Summary

To summarise, this final chapter has considered:

- an explanation of a systematic literature review and its differences to a dissertation or thesis literature review;
- the process of conducting a systematic literature review;
- the different approaches to synthesis and analysis of data which may be undertaken;
- a checklist of questions for the appraisal of a review.

A list of further reading is given below for more detailed information about systematic literature reviews.

Further reading

EPPI (Evidence for Policy and Practice Information) Centre http://www.eppi.ioe.ac.uk (accessed 11/04/12)

Higgins J.P.T. and Green, S. (eds) (2011) *Cochrane Handbook for Systematic Reviews of Interventions* Version 5.1.0 (updated March 2011). The Cochrane Collaboration www.cochrane-handbook.org (accessed 15/08/11).

Jesson, J.K., Matheson, L. and Lacey, F.M. (2011) *Doing Your Literature Review: Traditional and Systematic Techniques.* London: Sage.

Petticrew, M. and Roberts, H. (2006) *Systematic Reviews in the Social Sciences: A Practical Guide.* Oxford: Blackwell.

Popay, J., Roberts, H., Sowden, A., Petticrew, M., Arai, L., Britten, N., Rodgers, M. and Britten, N. with Rosen, K. and Duffy, S. (2006) *Guidance on the Conduct of Narrative Synthesis in Systematic Reviews: Final Report.* Swindon: ESRC Methods Programme http://www.lancs.ac.uk/shm/research/nssr/research/dissemination/publications.php (accessed 15/08/11).

Okoli, C. and Schabram, K. (2010) 'A guide to conducting a systematic literature review of information systems research', *Sprouts: Working Papers on Information Systems* 10 (26) http://sprouts.aisnet.org/10-26 (accessed 08/08/11).

RevMan (2008) Review Manager (RevMan) (Computer Program) Version 5.0 Copenhagen: The Nordic Cochrane Centre, The Cochrane Collaboration.

Rutter, D., Francis, J., Coren, E. and Fisher, M. (2010) *SCIE Systematic Research Reviews: Guidelines* (2nd edn). London: Social Care Institute for Excellence http://www.scie.org.uk/publications/researchresources/rr01.asp (accessed 15/08/11).

SCIE (Social Care Institute for Excellence) http://www.scie.org.uk (accessed 14/04/12)

The Campbell Collaboration http://www.campbellcollaboration.org/ (accessed 12/04/12)

The Cochrane Collaboration http://www.cochrane.org/ (accessed 14/04/12)

Torgerson, C. (2003) *Systematic Reviews,* London: Continuum.

Conclusion

In this book we have explored both the literature review process and product. I have emphasised the importance of the reading in relation to your research from the beginning until the end of your research project. Throughout the chapters, guidelines and suggestions have been put forward which encourage you to consider the way you approach your literature searches, the reading, the management of a personal library, the purposes of your literature review, and the integration of the literature into your writing. The many examples from different dissertations and theses have shown how writers can direct their own argument and achieve criticality through effective critical reading and the adoption of a variety of appropriate writing and citation techniques. The intention has been to provide – whatever the research context in which you are working – advice in the book which can be implemented in the specific environment of your discipline.

Despite the generic nature of much of the discussion in the book, the significance of disciplinary difference has been recognised and the extracts from dissertations and theses represent a range of different fields and approaches to research. Furthermore, while realising that many dissertations and theses follow the conventional structure, with its distinct literature review chapter or chapters, it has also been acknowledged that the nature of research in some fields lends itself to a more integrated approach where citations are interspersed throughout the whole dissertation or thesis. In the final chapter of this edition of the book, the discussion has expanded to explore the nature and role of a systematic literature review and the differences from a typical dissertation or thesis literature review. Although this type of review is usually carried out by a team of professional researchers, it is important for students undertaking research to have a full understanding of the purposes and procedures involved.

Whatever the specific context of your research, the literature can arouse your curiosity, extend your thinking and help you make sense of the issue you are grappling with as the particular focus of your enquiry. Hence, the literature review is a challenging but potentially very rewarding part of the research process which merits considerable nurturing and tender loving care. I hope that this book has offered ideas which can assist you in this endeavour.

Electronic guides

Websites

Associated Press (2006) DNA verifies Columbus' remains in Spain May 19th: http://www.msnbc. msn.com/id/12871458/ (accessed 11/06/11)
British Psychological Association: http://www.bps.org.uk/
CiteULike – social bookmarking site for discovering and managing references: http://www.citeulike.org/
Intellectual Property Office: http://www.ipo.gov.uk/
Oxfam: http://www.oxfam.org.uk/
Royal College of Nursing (RCN): http://www.rcn.org.uk/
The Chartered Institute of Public Finance and Accountancy (CIPFA): http://www.cipfa.org.uk/
The Copyright Licensing Agency: http://www.cla.co.uk/
The Department for Education: http://www.education.gov.uk/
The Institution of Engineering and Technology (IET): http://www.theiet.org/
The Law Society: http://www.lawsociety.org.uk/home.law
United Kingdom Literacy Association (UKLA): http://www.ukla.org/
Wikipedia: http://en.wikipedia.org/wiki/Main_Page

Reference management software

EndNote: http://www.endnote.com/
NVivo: http://www.qsrinternational.com/products_nvivo.aspx
ProCite: http://www.procite.com/
Reference Manager: http://www.refman.com/
RefWorks: http://www.refworks.com/

Note-taking software

Evernote – digital notebook: http://www.evernote.com/

Microsoft OneNote – digital notebook: http://office.microsoft.com/en-us/onenote/
Mind genius – mind mapping software: http://www.mindgenius.com/

Web pages for literature searches

Altavista Internet search engine: http://www.altavista.com/
Amazon online booksellers: http://www.amazon.co.uk
British Library Catalogues: http://www.bl.uk/catalogues/listings.html
BUBL catalogue of Internet resources: http://www.bubl.ac.uk/link/types/opacs.htm
Copac National, Academic and Specialist Library Catalogue: http://www.copac.ac.uk/
Directory of Open Access Journals (DOAJ): http://www.doaj.org/
Dissertation abstracts – US and worldwide dissertations and theses: http://library.dialog.com/bluesheets/html/bl0035.html
EPPI (Evidence for Policy and Practice Information) Centre – systematic reviews in social science and public policy: http://www.eppi.ioe.ac.uk
EthOS – the British Library's Electronic Thesis Online Service: http://ethos.bl.uk/
Google Internet search engine: http://www.google.com/
Google Scholar Internet search engine: http://scholar.google.com/
Index to UK theses: http://www.theses.com/
Library of Congress catalog: http://www.loc.gov/z3950/gateway.html
MEDLINE – journal abstracts for biomedical literature from around the world: http://www.nlm.nih.gov/bsd/pmresources.html
ProQuest – citations and abstracts for articles, ebooks and dissertations in a wide range of disciplines: http://www.proquest.co.uk/en-UK/
PubMed – open access database for biomedical literature: http://www.ncbi.nlm.nih.gov/pubmed/
Sage Publications: http://www.sage.co.uk/
ScienceDirect: http://www.sciencedirect.com
SCIE (Social Care Institute for Excellence) – systematic reviews in social care http://www.scie.org.uk
The Campbell Collaboration – systematic reviews in education, crime and justice and social welfare: http://www.campbellcollaboration.org/
The Cochrane Collaboration – systematic reviews in healthcare: http://www.cochrane.org/
Web of Knowledge – citations and abstracts for literature in the sciences, social sciences, arts and humanities: http://wok.mimas.ac.uk/
Zetoc – the British Library's electronic table of contents for current journals and conference proceedings: http://zetoc.mimas.ac.uk/index.html

Guidance on referencing and plagiarism

Massachusetts Institute of Technology *Academic Integrity at MIT* http://web.
mit.edu/academicintegrity/index.html (accessed 19/02/11)
Turnitin http://turnitin.com/static/products/index.php (accessed 9/4/11)
University of Southampton A Guide to Academic Integrity http://www.study
skills.soton.ac.uk/integrity/ (accessed 19/02/11)
University of Leicester *Avoiding Plagiarism: online tutorial* http://www2.le.
ac.uk/offices/ssds/sd/ld/resources/study/plagiarism-tutorial (accessed 19/02/11)

Web pages for copyright

The Copyright Licensing Agency   http://www.cla.co.uk/
Intellectual Property Office   http://www.ipo.gov.uk/

Web pages for systematic literature reviews

EPPI (Evidence for Policy and Practice Information) Centre http://www.eppi.
ioe.ac.uk
SCIE (Social Care Institute for Excellence) http://www.scie.org.uk
The Campbell Collaboration http://www.campbellcollaboration.org/
The Cochrane Collaboration http://www.cochrane.org/

References

Allam, C. (2005) 'Heinz 57 blended learning at the University of Sheffield: some case studies'. MEd dissertation, University of Sheffield.

Arai, L., Britten, N., Popay, J., Roberts, H., Petticrew, M., Rodgers, M. and Sowden, A. (2007) 'Testing methodological developments in the conduct of narrative synthesis: a demonstration review of research on the implementation of smoke alarm interventions', *Evidence and Policy*, 3 (3): 361–83.

Bacigalupo, R. (2000) 'The information management of health visitors: with particular reference to their public health and community development activities'. PhD thesis, University of Sheffield.

Bell, J. (2010) *Doing Your Research Project: A Guide for First-Time Researchers in Education, Health and Social Science* (5th edn). Maidenhead: Open University Press.

Blaxter, L., Hughes, C. and Tight, M. (2010) *How to Research* (4th edn). Buckingham: Open University Press.

Boaz, A., Ashby, D., Denyer, D., Egan, M., Harden, A., Jones, D.R., Pawson, R. and Tranfield, D. (2006) 'A multitude of syntheses: a comparison of five approaches from diverse policy fields', *Evidence and Policy*, 2 (4): 479–502.

Bruce, C.S. (1994) 'Research students' early experiences of the dissertation literature review', *Studies in Higher Education*, 19 (2): 217–29.

Brunton, G., Oliver, S., Oliver, K., and Lorenc, T. (2006) *A Synthesis of Research Addressing Children's, Young People's and Parents' Views of Walking and Cycling for Transport*. London: EPPI-Centre, Social Science Research Unit, Institute of Education, University of London.

Calcraft, R. (2004) 'Children left at home alone: The Construction of a social problem'. PhD thesis, University of Nottingham.

Coveney, E. (2003) 'A reassertion of value: a study of value as illustrated by conservation and regeneration in historic urban quarters: the Birmingham jewellery quarter and the Nottingham lace market'. MA dissertation, University of Sheffield.

Culverson, D.E. (2002) 'Exploring organizational commitment following radical change: a care study within the Parks Canada Agency'. MA dissertation. Ontario, Canada: University of Waterloo.

EPPI-Centre (March 2007) *EPPI-Centre methods for conducting systematic reviews*. London: EPPI-Centre, Social Science Research Unit, Institute of Education, University of London.

Fairbrother, H. (2010) 'Children, food and health'. MPhil to PhD Upgrade Report, University of Sheffield.

Fernandez, R. and Griffiths, R. (2010) *Water for wound cleansing*. Cochrane Database of Systematic Reviews 2010, Issue 1. Art. No. CD003861. DOI: 10.1002/14651858. CD003861.pub2.v http://onlinelibrary.wiley.com/doi/10.1002/14651858.CD003861.pub2/ abstract (accessed 09/10/11).

Feng, L. (2010) 'Education for sustainable development curricula: three case study Masters programmes in England and China'. PhD thesis, University of Sheffield.

Gash, S. (1999) *Effective Literature Searching for Research* (2nd edn). Aldershot: Gower Publishing Ltd.

Groom, N. (2000) 'Attribution and averral revisited: three perspectives on manifest intertextuality in academic writing', in P. Thompson (ed.), *Patterns and Perspectives: Insights into EAP Writing Practice*. Centre for Applied Language Studies: The University of Reading.

Hart, C. (1998) *Doing a Literature Review: Releasing the Social Science Research Imagination*. London: Sage Publications.

Harden, A. and Thomas, J. (2005) 'Methodological issues in combining diverse study types in systematic reviews', *International Journal of Social Research Methodology*, 8 (3): 257–71.

Hemilä, H., Chalker E. and Douglas B. (2007) *Vitamin C for preventing and treating the common cold*. Cochrane Database of Systematic Reviews 2007, Issue 3. Art. No.: CD000980. DOI: 10.1002/14651858.CD000980.pub3 http://www2.cochrane.org/reviews/en/ab000980.html (accessed 08/06/11).

Hemingway, P. and Brereton, N. (2009) 'What is a systematic review?' in *What is …? Series* (2nd edn). http://www.whatisseries.co.uk/whatis/pdfs/What_is_syst_rev.pdf (accessed 09/06/11).

Higgins J.P.T. and Green, S. (eds) (2011) *Cochrane Handbook for Systematic Reviews of Interventions* Version 5.1.0 (updated March 2011). The Cochrane Collaboration. http://www.cochrane-handbook.org/ (accessed 12/04/12).

Howard, R.M. (1995) 'Plagiarisms, authorships and the academic death penalty', *College English*, 57(7): 788–805.

Huffaker, D.A., and Calvert, S.L. (2005) 'Gender, identity, and language use in teenage blogs', *Journal of Computer-Mediated Communication,* 10 (2), article 1. http://jcmc.indiana.edu/vol10/ issue2/huffaker.html (accessed 17/06/06).

Hull, G. and Rose, M. (1989) 'Rethinking remediation: toward a social-cognitive understanding of problematic reading and writing', *Written Communication* 6(2): 139–154.

Hyland, K. (1999) 'Disciplinary discourses: writer stance in research articles', in C.N. Candlin and K. Hyland (eds), *Writing: Texts, Processes and Practices*. London: Longman.

Hyland, K. (2004) *Disciplinary Discourses: Social Interactions in Academic Writing*. Ann Arbor: The University of Michigan Press.

Ivanič, R. (1998) *Writing and Identity: The Discoursal Construction of Identity in Academic Writing*. Amsterdam: John Benjamins Publishing Company.

Jadad, A.R., Moore, R.A., Carroll, D., Jenkinson, C., Reynolds, D.J., Gavaghan, D.J. and McQuay, H.J. (1996) 'Assessing the quality of reports of randomized clinical trials: is blinding necessary?' *Controlled Clinical Trials*, 17 (1): 1–12.

Jesson, J.K., Matheson, L. and Lacey, F.M. (2011) *Doing Your Literature Review: Traditional and Systematic Techniques*. London: Sage Publications.

Lee, E. (2003) 'Language shift and revitalisation in the Kristang Community, Portuguese Settlement, Malacca'. PhD thesis, University of Sheffield.

Machi, L.A. and McEvoy, B.T. (2009) *The Literature Review*. Thousand Oaks, CA: Corwin Press.

Meyer, M. (2006) 'Partially connected to science: the Luxembourg Museum of Natural History and its scientific collaborators'. PhD thesis, University of Sheffield.

Moore, A. (2001) 'The effects of formal instruction on EFL pronunciation acquisition: a case study from Germany'. MA dissertation, University of Surrey.

Murray, R. (2011) *How to Write a Thesis* (3rd edn). Buckingham: Open University Press.

Nunan, D. (1992) *Research Methods in Language Learning*. Cambridge: Cambridge University Press.

Okoli, C. and Schabram, K. (2010) 'A guide to conducting a systematic literature review of information systems research', *Sprouts: Working Papers on Information Systems* 10 (26) http://sprouts.aisnet.org/10-26 (accessed 08/08/11).

Ovcina, D. (2010) 'The dynamics of market entry and expansion strategy in emerging markets: the case of Wal-Mart in Latin America'. MSc dissertation, Sheffield Hallam University.

Overton, S.E. (2002) 'Sustainable urban drainage systems (SUDS) – quality modelling'. Undergraduate dissertation, University of Sheffield.

Parker-Jenkins, M., Hewitt, D., Brownhill, S. and Sanders, T. (2004) 'What strategies can be used by initial teacher training providers, trainees and newly qualified teachers to raise the attainment of pupils from culturally diverse backgrounds?' in *Research Evidence in Education Library*. London: EPPI-Centre, Social Science Research Unit, Institute of Education, University of London.

Petticrew, M. and Roberts, H. (2006) *Systematic Reviews in the Social Sciences: A Practical Guide*. Oxford: Blackwell.

Phillips, P.M. and Pugh, D.S. (2010) *How to Get a PhD: A Handbook for Students and their Supervisors* (5th edn). Buckingham: Open University Press.

Popay, J., Roberts, H., Sowden, A., Petticrew, M., Arai, L., Britten, N., Rodgers, M. and Britten, N. with Rosen, K. and Duffy, S. (2006) Guidance on the Conduct of Narrative Synthesis in Systematic Reviews: Final Report. Swindon: ESRC Methods Programme http://www.lancs.ac.uk/shm/research/nssr/research/dissemination/publications.php (accessed 15/08/11).

RevMan (2008) Review Manager (RevMan) (Computer Program) Version 5.0 Copenhagen: The Nordic Cochrane Centre, The Cochrane Collaboration.

Rudestam, K.E. and Newton, R.R. (2007) *Surviving your Dissertation: A Comprehensive Guide to Content and Process* (3rd edn). Thousand Oaks, CA: Sage Publications Inc.

Rutter, D., Francis, J., Coren, E. and Fisher, M. (2010) *SCIE Systematic Research Reviews: Guidelines* (2nd edn). London: Social Care Institute for Excellence.

Son, Key-young (2004) 'South Korean identities in strategies of engagement with North Korea: a case study of President Kim Dae-jung's Sunshine Policy'. PhD thesis, University of Sheffield.

Swales, J.M. (1990) *Genre Analysis: English in Academic Research Settings*. Cambridge: Cambridge University Press.

Swales, J.M. and Feak, C.B. (2000) *English in Today's Research World: A Writing Guide*. Ann Arbor: The University of Michigan Press.

Swales, J.M. and Feak, C.B. (2004) *Academic Writing for Graduate Students: Essential Tasks and Skills* (2nd edn). Ann Arbor: The University of Michigan Press.

Tang, R. and John, S. (1999) 'The "I" in identity: exploring writer identity in student academic writing through the first person pronoun', English for Specific Purposes, 18: S21–S39. Reading: The Centre for Applied Language Studies, University of Reading.

Taylor, G. (1989) *The Student's Writing Guide for the Arts and Social Sciences*. Cambridge: Cambridge University Press.

The Campbell Collaboration (no date) *Producing a Review*. http://www.campbellcollabora tion.org/systematic_reviews/index.php (accessed 12/04/12).

Thomas, S. and Hawes, T.P. (1994) 'Reporting verbs in medical journal articles', *English for Specific Purposes*, 13 (2): 129–48.

Thompson, P. (ed.) (2000) *Patterns and Perspectives: Insights into EAP Writing Practice*. Reading: The Centre for Applied Language Studies, University of Reading.

Thompson, G. and Ye Yiyun (1991) 'Evaluation in the reporting verbs used in academic papers', *Applied Linguistics*, 12 (4): 365–82.

Torgerson, C.J., Brooks, G. and Hall J. (2006) *A Systematic Review of the Research Literature on the Use of Phonics in the Teaching of Reading and Spelling*. The University of Sheffield: DfES

Walliman, N. (2011) *Your Research Project: Designing and Planning your Work* (3rd edn). London: Sage Publications.

Watson, I.A. (2004) 'Modelling of natural attenuation processes in groundwater using adaptive and parallel numerical methods'. PhD thesis, University of Sheffield.

Webb, T. (2003) 'Motivational and volitional aspects of self-regulation'. PhD thesis, University of Sheffield.

Weissberg, R. and Buker, S. (1990) *Writing Up Research: Experimental Research Report Writing for Students of English*. Englewood Cliffs, NJ: Prentice Hall.

Wellington, J., Bathmaker, A., Hunt, C., McCulloch, G. and Sikes, P. (2005) *Succeeding With Your Doctorate*. London: Sage Publications.

Wenger, E. (1990) 'Toward a theory of cultural transparency: elements of a social discourse of the visible and the invisible'. PhD dissertation, University of California.

Wenger, E. (1998) *Communities of Practice: Learning, Meaning and Identity*. Cambridge: Cambridge University Press.

Woodgate, J.A. (2005) 'Self-efficacy theory and the self-regulation of exercise behaviour'. PhD thesis, University of Waterloo, Ontario, Canada.

Index